The
Brain
Power
Workout

The ■ Brain Power *Workout*

300 ways to improve your memory and creativity

Joel Levy

CICO BOOKS

LONDON NEW YORK

Published in 2010 by CICO Books
An imprint of Ryland Peters & Small Ltd

20–21 Jockey's Fields   519 Broadway, 5th Floor
London WC1R 4BW   New York, NY 10012

www.cicobooks.com

10 9 8 7 6 5 4 3 2 1

Text © Joel Levy 2010
Design and illustrations © CICO Books 2010

A CIP catalog record for this book is available from the Library of Congress
and the British Library.

ISBN 978 1 907030 12 3

Printed in China

Editor: Robin Gurdon
Designer: Jerry Goldie
Illustrations: Trina Dalziel

Contents

Introduction

The human brain is perhaps the most extraordinary part of our body—the immensely powerful controller of every aspect of our existence. It is our brain's size and complexity that differentiates us from all other animals, including our closest relatives among the primates, and has allowed us to develop into the modern creatures we are today.

All that power, though, is little understood and is very underused. This book aims to change that by teaching you how to make the most of this incredible asset, honing your intelligence and increasing your memory capacity, until you can take on your daily life with renewed confidence and vigor.

This book is organized into four parts: How You Think, How You Remember, The Brain Power Lifestyle, and Challenges and Exercises.

How You Think

Part One explains how the brain works, so you will learn how its different parts function and interrelate, and discover how intelligence can be used and channeled through learning and the use of IQ tests.

One of the mysteries of the brain that has long puzzled scientists is exactly what intelligence is, how it can be measured, whether IQ is the right approach, and what IQ tests measure. We look at the IQ tests themselves—how they have evolved, how they produce your IQ score, what mental abilities they are actually testing, and what your IQ score means for you. Next, we consider the intriguing question of whether there is one broad, underlying intelligence or multiple, unrelated types of intelligence. We then look at how important and relevant IQ really is, and finally we examine some of the most controversial aspects of all—how much IQ is affected by genes, race, class, gender, and socioeconomic factors.

How You Remember

In Part Two, we explore the various types of memory and learn the practical skills of improving your recall—you'll amaze yourself with the amount of information you can keep at the front of your mind, with practice. Although there are still many mysteries about how we remember things, advances in research over the last decade and a half have provided new insights into the neurology and psychology of memory. Improving memory skills has also become more crucial than ever before, despite the fact that computers and other devices can carry out a lot of the hard labor of modern life. While technology can help you to access raw data, it cannot help you remember what you need to know or how it fits together.

What's more, digital technology has itself created new memory challenges (not least how to gain access to it in the first place, via PINs and passwords). In addition, your chances of living to a ripe old age are higher than ever, which means facing issues of memory health, such as age-related memory loss. The best approach, therefore, is to boost your memory power now and to keep it boosted.

The Brain Power Lifestyle

This section looks at our lifestyle and its impact on how the brain works, along with tips on supporting your recall ability, concentration, creativity, and more through good sleep habits and getting good nutrition, such as the impact of micronutrients like beta-carotene which help support memory. Also, discover the benefits of flexing your brain's mental muscles with tests and quizzes.

Challenges and Exercises

Throughout the book, chapters are interspersed with exercises and strategies to help improve the different areas of your brain function—to raise it to a level when you can have the confidence that you are using your greatest asset to its full potential. Part Four presents an intensive selection of questions, brainteasers, riddles, and IQ tests to test how far you have progressed and also keep your new-found skills at the peak of their abilities—like any muscle in the body, if you don't keep the brain exercised it will begin to lose its ability to perform to the highest standard.

Your brain is your gateway to the world. Put it to use in the most productive way you can and see your life improve with it!

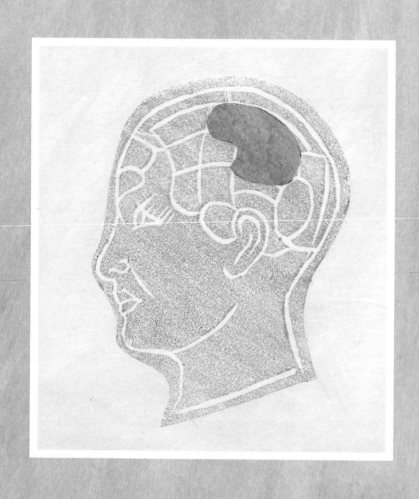

Part One

How You Think

How Are You Wired?

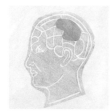

Cradled inside your skull is an unprepossessing lump of pinky-gray tissue, weighing about 3 lb (1.3 kg). It's not much to look at, but this "lump" is the seat of emotion, reason, memory, language, logic, sensation, will, and consciousness. It regulates and directs your body's basic processes, controls your actions, and generates every aspect of your inner life. In this section, we look at the biology that makes this possible, starting with the basic cellular building blocks of the nervous system, and working up to the structure and organization of the brain.

The neuron

The building block of the brain and the rest of the nervous system is the nerve cell, or neuron. Your brain contains over 100 billion of these, connected in webs of indescribable complexity.

Structure of the neuron

Neurons are extremely unusual cells. Although the main body of the nerve cell is as small as most other cells, the overall length of the cell may be more than three feet, thanks to the long projections that lead out from the cell body. Neurons in the brain may have dozens of these projections, called dendrites, each of which can split into smaller branches. This allows a single neuron to make contact with up to 50,000 others, collecting information from other neurons and bringing it to the cell body. One dendrite, much longer than the others, is the axon, which can stretch up to 3 ft (1 m) before branching to make contact with the dendrites of other neurons. In most neurons the axon is coated with a fatty white sheath called myelin, which acts as a kind of insulator, speeding the transmission of nervous signals.

Function of the neuron

The neuron is like a tiny biological microprocessor chip. It collects inputs from other neurons (via the dendrites), processes them (in the cell body), and gives an output (via

Neuron

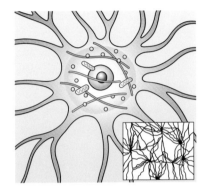

Neurons pass nervous signals to each other through the body using vast webs of dendrites.

Synapse

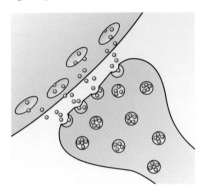

At the end of each dendrite is the synapse—the gap across which signals are passed to the next neuron.

the axon). The neuron is able to accomplish this because it is electrically charged. By transporting ions across its cell membrane it builds up an electrical potential between the inside and the outside. If the neuron receives enough inputs, a change in the cell membrane is triggered, causing rapid discharge of the electrical potential along its entire length, producing the traveling electrical impulse commonly known as a nervous signal.

Synapses

Nervous signals—the inputs and outputs of neuron function—are transmitted between neurons at a synapse, which is where the axon of one neuron connects to the dendrite of another, separated only by a tiny synaptic gap. When a nerve signal arrives at the end of the axon, small packets of special chemicals, known as neurotransmitters, are released into the gap and are picked up by receptor proteins on the other side. If enough signals are picked up, it generates its own electrical impulse and propagates the nervous signal.

Neurotransmitters

Different transmitters are used by different types of neurons, or are in different areas of the brain, or they may have differing effects on the same neuron—some will excite the neuron, others will inhibit it, making it less likely to fire. Neurotransmitters play a vital role in controlling brain processes.

By altering the subtle balance of neurotransmitters in the brain, through the use of pharmaceutical or recreational drugs, for instance, it is possible to affect mood, motor control, perception, memory, and even consciousness itself. For example, the neurotransmitter serotonin plays a major role in the production and regulation of emotions and mood. Serotonin levels change over the course of the day and the year, can be affected by the food you eat, and are modified by antidepressants like Prozac and drugs like Ecstasy.

The central nervous system

The brain is just one element in the nervous system, which can be divided up in many ways. The peripheral nervous system includes the nerves that lead to and from the different parts of your body, including the nerves that signal heat felt on the back of the hand, or that trigger the contraction of your calf muscles. The central nervous system includes the spine, the brain stem, the cerebellum, and the cerebrum.

Basic divisions of the brain

The spine comes up through the base of the skull and swells into the most primitive part of the brain, the brain stem.

- The brain stem controls the unconscious processes of the body, such as breathing, and whether you are awake or asleep. All nerve signals between the brain and the body and senses, incoming and outgoing, pass through this region, and it is also where nerve signals from the right-hand side of your body cross over to lead to the left-hand side of the brain, and vice versa.

- The cerebellum sits at the base of the brain and controls the complex programs of neuronal firing needed to produce smooth, coordinated, and balanced movement. While you may consciously decide to walk using higher parts of the brain, it is the cerebellum that actually carries out the neural processes involved.

- The cerebrum is what most people mean when they talk about the brain. This is where all your higher mental functions, like thinking, memory, and language, reside, and is also the seat of consciousness. In most other animals, it is much smaller and less developed. The outer surface of the cerebrum, called the cerebral cortex, is deeply wrinkled and fissured so that it looks like a walnut. The extensive wrinkling allows more of it to fit into the skull.

- Between the cerebrum and lower parts of the brain are "in-between" structures that link the conscious processes of the cerebrum to the unconscious processes of the brain stem: the thalamus, hypothalamus, and limbic system. They are involved in generating and regulating the "animal" parts of your personality—your emotions, fears, and basic drives, such as hunger, thirst, and sexual desire. They are also involved in learning and memory formation.

The cerebral hemispheres

The cerebrum itself is divided into two halves, known as the left and right cerebral hemispheres. Although the two hemispheres are anatomically almost identical, they perform different roles. In most people, the left hemisphere is dominant for functions such as language, logic, and mathematical ability, while the right hemisphere is dominant for emotions, art, and spatial reasoning. Each hemisphere controls the sensory and motor functions of the opposite side of the body, but in most people the left hemisphere is dominant for motor control, making them right-handed.

Right- and left-brain differences

You are not normally conscious of any of this separation of roles, thanks to the corpus callosum, a bridge of neural fibers that connects the two hemispheres, providing a high-speed information transfer link. Messages pass so quickly between the hemispheres that they are able to operate as a single unit.

It is, however, possible to pick up on the difference between the hemispheres by testing your immediate reaction to asymmetrical stimuli. For instance, make an instant decision about which of the faces below looks happier to you.

Even though the pictures are simply mirror images of one another, the majority of

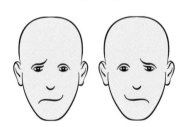

people pick the right-hand one. Because the right hemisphere is dominant for emotion, it is the information in the left field of vision that has the most immediate impact on your perception of emotion—in this case, it's the right-hand picture, where the smile is to the left of the nose (i.e., in the left field of vision).

One-sided people

Occasionally, through stroke, injury, or surgery, one hemisphere of the brain is damaged while the other continues to function. People afflicted in this way can display a condition known as unilateral neglect, where they appear to be unable to perceive or think about one side of space. Symptoms include putting all the numbers in one half when drawing a clock face, as above; eating only half of the food on a plate (if the plate is turned

around, the subject is able to eat the other half); and even failing to recognize limbs on the affected side.

Lobes of the brain

Each hemisphere is further divided into four lobes:

- The frontal lobes are at the front of the brain. They deal with the most "intellectual" functions, such as planning, forethought, strategy, will, and self-control. They also contain the main site of voluntary muscle control—the motor cortex—and some language control areas.

- The temporal lobes are on either side of the brain. They are involved in hearing, smell, and making sense of language. Disturbances (such as epilepsy) of this part of the brain are linked to frightening sensations, such as feeling menacing presences, or hearing preternatural sounds.

- The parietal lobes, across the top of the brain, contain the main area of sensory cortex, where sensations from different parts of the body are consciously felt.

- The occipital lobes at the back of the brain are mainly concerned with vision.

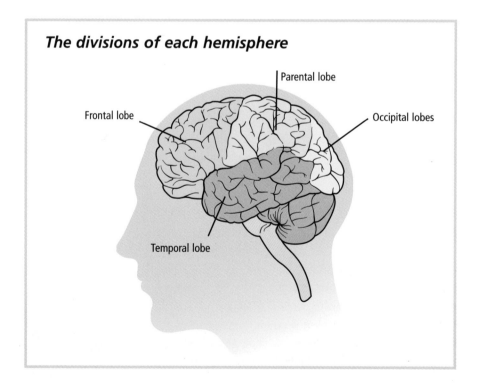

The divisions of each hemisphere

Parental lobe

Frontal lobe

Occipital lobes

Temporal lobe

Gender differences in the brain

It's widely assumed that there are major differences between male and female thinking, and therefore male and female brains. In practice, however, there are very few differences between the two, and even a trained anatomist would be hard put to tell the difference between two brains of different gender but equal size. On the whole, men's brains tend to be bigger and heavier, but this is probably because men tend to be bigger and heavier.

Cognitive differences between men and women

Nonetheless, some differences between male and female minds have been discovered. Women seem to be better, on average, at some verbal tasks and at multi-tasking (e.g., doing one thing while talking about another) but fare slightly worse than men at some tests of spatial reasoning, such as mentally rotating three-dimensional images. Men are also slightly better, on average, at some tests of navigation/map-reading, which conforms to a popular gender stereotype. It is very important to note, however, that these findings show that the average differences between the sexes are much smaller than the average differences between individuals—in other words, the map-reading abilities of any two men are likely to be just as different as those of a given man and woman.

The brain through life

The development of the brain begins early in pregnancy—within five weeks of conception the tiny fetus has a proto-spinal cord, which is swollen at the head end where the cerebrum will develop. Between weeks 9 and 12 the fetal brain and nerves start to function, and by week 20, when the fetus is just 7½ in (19 cm) long, it can react to sounds (although this does not mean it has yet developed any conscious awareness of them).

Whittling down the brain

Right from the start of pregnancy, the fetal brain cells are speedily replicating and increasing in number. By the time a baby is born, he or she has more neurons than at any point in the rest of his/her life. Over the next few years, many of these cells are "pruned away," to give the brain its fully functional form. Only those cells that are used remain—these get bigger and forge increasing numbers of connections with other cells. The number of support cells, which help to nurture and protect neurons, also grows; an adult has up to 50 times as many support cells as neurons (that's up to 5,000 billion).

Making connections

As an infant soaks up information about the world and him, or herself, billions of new synaptic connections are made. Until around the age of seven, a child's brain is especially pliable and can be rewired on a massive scale. After this age, neurons are rapidly coated with their fatty myelin sheaths, increasing the speed of transmission they can achieve, but limiting their ability to make new connections as quickly. This is what makes childhood such a critical phase for learning. The richer a child's environment and intellectual stimulation, the more connections his or her neurons can make, and the more powerful the brain becomes.

The aging brain

Some areas of the brain undergo additional growth during puberty and the teenage years, but after this, changes happen on a microscopic scale, as the number and pattern of synaptic connections are modified through learning and experience. There are over 100 trillion connections in your brain. Neurons continue to die off, however, and by late adulthood you are losing more than 100,000 nerve cells a day. Compared with the total this is a small proportion, but over the course of your adult life you can expect to lose about 7 percent of your brain cells.

Aging brings gradual changes in the brain—the cortex gets thinner, and fluid-filled spaces called ventricles enlarge slightly. However, neither of these changes actually affects your brain power very much. More serious is the decline in blood supply to the brain, which can slow it down and make it vulnerable to blood clots (causing strokes). The brain also becomes more vulnerable to degenerative diseases such as Alzheimer's, where plaques of protein build up around some neurons, interfering with their function and reducing the density of connections they can make.

Rejuvenating the brain

The good news is that there are plenty of things you can do to minimize age-related decline and maximize your mental powers. Exercise and healthy living can maintain blood supply to the brain and protect it against damaging agents, while mental exercise, such as learning, being creative, or undertaking intellectual challenges, can maintain and increase the density of synaptic connections in the brain. The next two sections show you how to achieve this and boost your brain power.

Intelligence and Forward Thinking

Intelligence is defined as the ability to learn from experience, acquire knowledge, think abstractly, and adapt to your environment. Intelligence is not the same as knowledge, learning, or ability, though it can improve all three.

How does intelligence work?

Popular conceptions of intelligence are revealed by the phrases people use to describe it—"the ability to figure things out," "how quick or smart you are," "how well you do at school." But when psychologists try to define intelligence they run into trouble, because it quickly becomes obvious that it's a broad concept that covers many different things. One explanation for this is that there are many different types of intelligence.

Types of intelligence

Different theories describe different types of intelligence. According to one theory there are just two types: crystalized intelligence, which is knowledge that someone has acquired, and fluid intelligence, which is their ability to use this knowledge. According to another theory there are three types of intelligence: abstract intelligence—the ability to work with symbols; concrete intelligence—the ability to work with objects; and social intelligence—the ability to understand and relate to people. Other theories describe anything up to dozens of types; psychologist Robert Steinberg suggests three, while leading theorist Howard Gardner posits seven. Many of these theories, however, are really describing the same things but giving them different names.

Spatial, numerical, and verbal intelligence

Intelligence tests typically measure the more abstract aspects of intelligence. If you look at the IQ-style tests on pages 132–134, you'll see that the questions are divided up into categories that differ in fairly obvious ways. Some have to do with your ability to think about shapes and mentally manipulate them in space—known as spatial intelligence. Questions that deal with numbers and mathematics test what is known as numerical intelligence.

Other items ask you about words, and involve what is known as verbal intelligence. While verbal intelligence is an important element of intelligence tests, it is also one aspect of a wider area of mental functioning—communication, which includes language and non-verbal communication.

Emotional intelligence

One aspect of intelligence that used to be neglected, but is now a hot topic of research, is emotional intelligence. This is basically the same as social intelligence, and describes your ability to perceive, understand, and manage your own and other people's emotions, motivations, feelings, and concerns. It is also sometimes described as inter- or intra-personal intelligence.

Basic intelligence—the g factor

Different people perform better in tests of some types of intelligence and worse in others. Your own experience probably backs this up. For instance, you probably know people who are good with numbers but not so good at dealing with people (i.e., they have high numerical intelligence but low emotional intelligence). But is there a common factor that links all the different types of intelligence, and maybe even underlies them all?

Statistical tests on people's scores across all the different types of intelligence tests seem to show that there is a common factor—in other words, that someone who is good at a verbal test is more likely to also be good at a mathematical test. This common factor has been called g, for "general intelligence." g is a measure of someone's raw mental power.

A useful analogy is with race cars. Different cars might have different handling abilities, wheel and tire types, etc., so some cars do better in rallies on stock-car tracks while others perform better on a race track. The different handling characteristics,

tire types, and so on are comparable to a person's ability to deal with different types of problems—e.g., verbal vs. emotional problems.

One factor that will boost the performance of all the cars, whatever their differences, is a more powerful engine. g is the equivalent of engine power. Just as a race car with a more powerful engine is likely to win more races, so a person with a higher level of g is more likely to be successful in their career, academic achievements, and so on.

Where is intelligence located?

Because there is little agreement about exactly what constitutes intelligence, it's hard to say where in the brain it is located. If we think about intelligence as a constellation of different mental functions and abilities, then we can say that it is distributed all over the brain, but primarily in the cortex, the wrinkled outer layer of the brain. More specific abilities can be more precisely located—for instance, the most abstract mental functions, such as logical reasoning and forward planning, are primarily localized in the prefrontal cortex.

The location of g—if it exists at all—is an intriguing mystery. It is unlikely, however, simply to be a property of one part of the brain, and is most likely, instead, to relate to a general feature of brain process, such as the speed of transmission of nervous impulses along your neurons, or an innate tendency of your neurons to make connections more or less easily.

What's your IQ?

Intelligence is usually measured with tests that give a score called an intelligence quotient (IQ), and are therefore known as IQ tests. Although your score on an IQ test is a good indicator of past and future success in life, there are drawbacks to this method of assessing intelligence. (See pages 47–55.)

Forward planning

Related to many of the components of intelligence discussed above is the ability to forward plan—to assess future challenges, and plan responses and problem-solving strategies accordingly. This is considered to be

Goal checklist ✔

Your intelligence and forward-thinking faculties affect most aspects of your life, so you should be able to measure your progress in many different fields. However, progress will be in small increments at most, and it's unrealistic to expect big leaps in performance. You should be looking to hone your abilities.

After several months of intelligence workouts, aim to:

- ☐ Improve your score in general knowledge tests, and by a few points in IQ tests
- ☐ Complete brainteaser puzzles faster
- ☐ Be reading more challenging books and newspapers
- ☐ Be viewing more challenging TV
- ☐ Work out bills and expenses without a calculator
- ☐ Benefit from better performance at work—for example, through sharper analysis, working through reports faster, and grasping new projects and systems more easily

another of mankind's "highest" mental functions. Forward planning is the mental function involved in everything from chess playing and card games to business planning and deciding where you're going on vacation.

Boosting your intelligence and planning abilities

Abilities such as intelligence and forward planning are probably the most recently evolved aspects of human psychology, which makes them both fragile and flexible. According to Gamon and Bragdon, in a recent book, "[these] functions are the most malleable and improvable with practice." In other words, giving your highest faculties a workout can help to sharpen them and keep them sharp.

Go to page 132 for a series of exercises to test and improve the different areas of your intelligence and forward thinking

Creativity and Lateral Thinking

Creativity is usually described as the ability to make new or unexpected connections between things, a quality that is technically known as divergent thinking or, more familiarly, lateral thinking. For instance, when divergent thinkers solve problems they explore different pathways of thinking, come up with new theories and interpretations, and look at things in unexpected ways.

By contrast, uncreative or convergent thinkers solve problems by following tried and tested paths of thought that they expect to "converge" on the single, correct solution. Once they solve a problem successfully, they expect all similar problems to conform to the same pattern: They are said to have developed a mental set. Mental sets don't just apply to problems—you can develop a mental set about many different types of things, from how you expect people in certain occupations to behave, to how a tool can be used. This may limit your ability to deal with people, things, or ideas creatively.

Why is our thinking usually limited?

Convergent thinking sounds bad, but humans have evolved to think like this for a reason. In a complex world that throws up constant challenges, your success, and sometimes your very survival, depends on dealing with these challenges quickly and effectively. Our minds have evolved to take mental shortcuts so that we can do this.

If you are faced with a large, angry-looking creature that you don't recognize, but which is baring its fangs at you, there's no time to think creatively about what it might be, or how it might behave. You have to fall back on your mental shortcuts—in this case, the mental set that says, "Big, ugly creatures baring their fangs are dangerous, and probably want to eat me: I'd better not stick around!" Mostly this sort of convergent thinking works well enough, but it can limit your ability to think creatively. In today's world creative thinking is at a premium, so it pays to examine the habits of people who can think this way.

How creative thinkers work

Research has shown that people who are good at thinking creatively don't necessarily have high IQs. Instead, there are three particular personality characteristics that seem to be more important. The first is nonconformity—openness to experience, willingness to take risks or try new things, and lack of concern about conforming to accepted standards.

The second is curiosity. Creative thinkers constantly question, inspect, seek, and probe. This is partly because they are open to novelty (an aspect of nonconformity), but they are also more likely to notice new things, or to spot contradictions or flaws in accepted ways of doing things. When they do notice these, they don't simply accept them, but feel compelled to investigate further.

Finally, although it may sound like a stereotype, creative people display persistence; hence the old adage, often attributed to Albert Einstein, "Genius is ten percent inspiration and ninety percent perspiration."

Creative people worry at problems until they find the solution, and may even go further, being unwilling to accept the obvious or conventional solution.

Situational factors (also known as circumstances) also boost creativity. People become more creative when they are in a good mood and are allowed to work without pressure and supervision. Your motivation also makes a difference—if you are motivated to achieve creativity for its own ends, you are more likely to do so than if seeking to serve an ulterior purpose (for instance, making money).

Boosting your creativity and problem-solving abilities

Learning to think creatively can make you better at solving all kinds of problems. The two key principles are learning to think out of the box, and developing a receptive mental state.

Thinking out of the box

Creative, also known as lateral, thinking is thinking that allows new or unexpected associations to be created between objects or people. This is only possible if you can overcome the old and conventional mental sets that usually restrict thinking. A

The candle problem

A good illustration of thinking out of the box is the candle problem, where two groups are challenged to mount a candle on the side of a vertical screen. One group is given a small candle, a box of matches, and a thumbtack. The other group is given the same materials, but with the matches outside of the box. The first group typically struggles with this problem, but the second group much more quickly works out the solution: to tack the inner tray of the matchbox onto the screen and mount the candle on the matchbox.

The first group struggled because of functional fixedness—because the box contained matches, they could not think of it in any other way than as a container. The second group was able to overcome this because, when the box did not contain the matches, it was easier to think of as a support.

good example of this sort of restrictive mental set is the concept of "functional fixedness." Functional fixedness is where our concept of an object, and how it can be used or what it can be used for, is restricted by the roles and functions most often associated with that object.

Brainstorming is a strategy used to encourage creativity. The idea is that by telling people to come up with any idea, no matter how dumb it sounds, you encourage them to break free of mental sets and think out of the box. Group brainstorming offers the further bonus of feedback, where divergent thinking by one person can be taken further by another.

Receptive state of mind

Many people find that the solution to a problem comes to them when they stop trying to think about the problem—in fact, when they are not thinking about anything at all. It's at times such as dropping off to sleep, engaging in an almost automatic task (e.g., driving, doing the washing-up), or simply winding down at the end of the day, that the most vivid imagery or original ideas can occur. These are precisely the times when the human mind is at its most receptive, because there are no distracting thoughts. Conversely, stress, noise, pressure, and distraction all hamper creativity.

Achieving a receptive state of mind means learning to shut off distracting thoughts and outside perceptions, and quiet your physiological as well as mental state. These are the same techniques that are used in meditation and relaxation.

Goal checklist ✔

Strangely enough, developing greater creativity requires effort, which is usually seen as an opposing quality. But creativity is a mental habit, and changing existing mental habits is hard work, and can only be achieved by consciously practicing skills that you hope will become unconscious.

By working at the strategies and exercises outlined in the book you should get better at:

☐ Making unusual or new connections between things

☐ Arranging information in new or unusual ways

☐ Solving problems in new ways, or with solutions from different types of problem

☐ Coming up with ideas in meetings

☐ Expressing yourself in unusual or effective ways, specially through the use of analogies

Emotional intelligence

Emotional intelligence is the ability to perceive and understand your own and other people's emotions, motivations, feelings, and concerns, and to use this information to guide your thinking and actions. Though the concept has only become popular relatively recently, it dates back many years.

Social intelligence

As far back as 1920, psychologist E. L. Thorndike described what he called "social intelligence," which he defined as the ability to understand and relate to people. Later, social intelligence was used to explain the evolution of the human brain—according to some theories, humans evolved larger brains as the result of their developing social skills. The more advanced their social abilities became, the more complex human society became, and the greater the need for still better social intelligence, and hence larger brains.

The importance of emotional intelligence

During the 1990s psychologists grew to appreciate that social intelligence applied not just to interpersonal interactions (interactions between people) but also to intrapersonal processes (internal mental processes), and coined the term "emotional intelligence" (EI) to cover all aspects of this ability. Research showed that EI plays an important role, not just in relationships but also in the workplace, classroom, and any other sphere where people interact or emotions come into play. On a more personal level, your levels of EI also determine:

- How well you know yourself
- How well you can communicate your needs and feelings
- How well you deal with conflict
- The extent to which you can transform patterns of thinking and behavior so you can grow as a person

People with high levels of EI are more likely to be self-aware, confident, balanced, and fulfilled, and are also better at dealing with other people. They make good salespeople, managers, team workers, and leaders, and also do well in the caring professions such as medicine and other jobs where interaction and sympathy for other people is vital.

Components of EI
There are many different ways to divide up EI into its component abilities. According to Professor Jack Mayer and Dr. Peter Salovey, the leading researchers and theorizers in the field, emotional intelligence can be divided into five distinct and separate domains:

Self-awareness: Observing yourself and recognizing feelings as they happen

Managing emotions: Handling feelings so that they are expressed and acted on appropriately; realizing what is behind a feeling; finding ways to cope with fear, anxiety, anger, and sadness

Motivating yourself: Using emotions to help achieve goals; self control; delaying gratification; overcoming damaging impulses

Empathy: Sensitivity to other people's feelings and concerns; being able to see things from their perspective; appreciating differences in other people's viewpoints

Handling relationships: Managing emotions in others; social skills; the ability to handle conflict and difficult issues

Goal checklist ✔

Like IQ, your EI levels are largely set by adulthood, but you should be able to improve your emotional performance, especially by practicing the strategies and exercises outlined in the book, until they become second nature.

In particular, by improving your EI, you should get better at:

☐ Keeping your temper

☐ Remaining reasonable in high-pressure situations

☐ Not taking out your irritability on others

☐ Coping with other people's irritability

☐ Getting what you want from store salespeople, call-center operatives, waiters, and others

☐ Getting on with colleagues and your boss

☐ Avoiding arguments

EQ: Measuring your EI

To provide a tool for objectively quantifying EI, some psychologists have developed standardized tests that give a rating similar to IQ, which has naturally been dubbed "EQ" (emotional quotient). Such tests typically comprise inventories of statements to which you give ratings, multiple-choice-style questions, and visual recognition of emotions in faces. The EQ-style test on pages 136–137 combines some of these elements to give you a tool for assessing your own EI.

Can you boost your EQ?

As with IQ, psychologists disagree over the extent to which genetics or the environment determines EQ, and therefore how easy it is to improve a low EQ. Even if it is difficult to alter your underlying EI abilities, you can learn to work around a low EI with strategies that improve your emotional "performance." These strategies include making implicit emotional cues more explicit; observing the habits of emotionally intelligent people; and practicing emotional skills.

Go to page 135 for a series of exercises to test and improve the different areas of your creativity, lateral thinking and emotional intelligence.

Language and Communication

One of the hallmarks of human intelligence is that it creates its own cultural and social context. It does this through communication, and in particular through the use of language. Language is one of the most complex and advanced cognitive abilities, and yet children too young to use the bathroom or tie their own shoes seem to master it without effort.

But language, in the classic sense of verbal communication, is not the whole story. Nonverbal forms of communication supplement, and sometimes even subvert, spoken words. In this chapter we'll look at both, and show how you can develop your communication skills and keep your mind sharp.

Language in the brain

Like most complex/higher mental functions, language involves many different parts of the brain, depending on the exact task in question—usually several at once. However, three areas are particularly important:

- Broca's area: This is named for the French surgeon who discovered its function in 1861 by studying people who had damage to this part of the brain, and who showed a characteristic dysfunction, now known as Broca's aphasia. It is located on the posterior surface of the left frontal lobe (just about underneath the temple). It controls the production of language and is responsible for fluency and grammar.

- Wernicke's area: Named for a German neurologist, this is located just next to Broca's area, but on the temporal and parietal lobes, nearer the back of the head (just about above the ear). It controls meaning in language and converting sounds into mental concepts, and is responsible for comprehension of spoken and written language.

- The insula: This is an area below the surface of the brain, pretty well between Broca's and Wernicke's areas. It controls the actual mechanics of speech, such as pronunciation, timing, and order.

Together, these three areas help us to formulate, understand, and speak language. Other parts of the brain that are important are those that deal with memory—important for remembering meanings, spelling and some grammar, and word forms; the senses—especially hearing for speech and vision for body language and writing; and motor skills—for operating the vocal cords, tongue, and mouth.

How language develops

Children pick up language in the natural course of their development, and they seem to do it in much the same way around the world, no matter what language they are learning. Although they are obviously not born able to write and speak, they are equipped with a built-in language-acquisition device. This is an innate ability to absorb language from parents and other adults, and to automatically develop vocabulary, grammar, and all the other elements that make someone a fluent speaker.

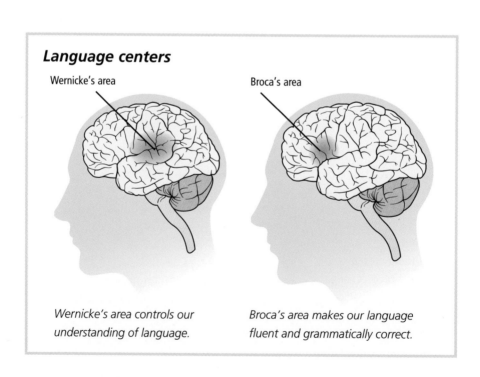

Language centers

Wernicke's area

Broca's area

Wernicke's area controls our understanding of language.

Broca's area makes our language fluent and grammatically correct.

Stages in language formation

From around the age of four to six months infants start to make vocalizations such as coos, grunts, and sounds similar to vowels and consonants. From six months to about a year, infants reach the babbling stage. Babies from all over the world, and even deaf babies, seem to babble in the same way, suggesting that the tendency to do so is hardwired into the child. After about a year children start to form actual words and by age three they progress to clauses, reaching properly grammatical speech at around age four.

The progress and degree of development of each stage depends on interaction with caregivers. Children learn by repeating sounds and words made by adults, and from the feedback that adults give to them. The more parents communicate with children, the more language they pick up.

The critical window

The automatic language-acquisition device seems to stay in operation until around the age of 12, over a period known as the critical window for language development. After puberty, this ability is lost, possibly because the neurons in the post-pubertal brain aren't able to make new connections so quickly. This is why it is much easier for children to pick up languages than adults. After this age, learning new languages seems to involve different parts of the brain from the parts that deal with genuinely fluent use of language, so a late learner may never become truly fluent.

Nonverbal communication

Even before they start to develop their verbal skills, infants can respond to and initiate nonverbal forms of communication, such as smiling, eye widening, nose wrinkling, following others' glances, and pointing fingers. Debate rages over whether expressions such as smiles, frowns, and nose wrinkles (to display disgust) are learned or innate, but they are universal across human cultures, so that your answers to the expression-matching test in Part 4 (Emotional Intelligence) would be the same as those of a Xhosa bushman or a New Guinea forest dweller.

Body language

Facial expressions are perhaps the most obvious form of nonverbal communica-tion. A more subtle form is body language. The way that you stand, sit, or lean,

Body language instant vocabulary interpreter

Body language is very useful for spotting lying, interest, flirtation, and so on, because unconscious gestures can undermine spoken words. Each gesture is a signal that you can decode. Carry the cards with you in public places to analyze strangers, then use them at work and at play to understand friends and colleagues. You can also assess body language in terms of emotional intelligence, see the human safari exercise on page 139.

When observing body language, focus on the following areas of the body:

- The eyes—particularly gaze and pattern of gaze movement

- The face—particularly expression and relation of hand to face

- The hands—particularly gestures and interaction with each other/use to highlight other points of body

- The arms and legs—particularly whether they are crossed

- The overall stance—whether standing or sitting

Approval
Two-hand handshake: Approval, interest, conveying warmth, and a desire to impress.

Leaning toward someone: Indication of liking or approval.

Defense
Arm crossing: Guarding behavior that indicates defensiveness or reservations.

Leg crossing also indicates defensiveness or reservations.

Receptivity
Hand steepling (pointing downward): Listening, receptivity, confidence.

Confidence
Hand steepling (pointing upward): Confidence, superiority, desire to show wisdom.

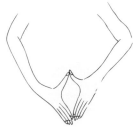

Openness
Open palms: Honesty, openness, nothing to hide.

Submission
Upturned palms, hands open: Acquiescence, pleading.

Disapproval
Down-facing palms, hands open: Dominance, control, disapproval.

Aggression
Palm closed, finger pointing: Aggression, command.

Friendship
Handshake with wrist grip: Sincerity, friendliness; may indicate opposite if used inappropriately.

Handshake with upper arm grab: Intimacy, empathy, support; may indicate opposite if used inappropriately.

Anticipation
Hand clench: Defensiveness, frustration.

Palm rubbing: Positive expectation.

Interest
Hand on cheek, index finger extended: Interest, receptivity.

Boredom
Hand on cheek, index finger extended, thumb under chin: Critical view, boredom.

Flirtation—men
Thumbs hooked over waistband:
Desire to appear confident,
assertive; displaying sexual
availability,
attraction.

Flirtation—women
Heel drop: Desire to
appear confident,
assertive; displaying
sexual availability,
attraction.

Lying
Nose touching or rubbing:
Concealing mouth.

Mouth covering—with
whole hand or just
a finger: Often
accompanied by
a cough.

Deceit
Ear rub or pull.

Eye rub, with eyes shut.

Concealment
Lack of facial and body mobility
may show that speaker is aware
of signals that can give the
game away and wants to
prevent them.

what you do with your arms, legs, hands, and feet, where you look, when and how often you move, and how you do all of these things in relation to other people—these are all means of communicating, or ways of passing on information about your mental and emotional state, motivations, and reservations. Some of the main categories of meaning signaled by body language are dominance/submission, attraction/dislike, agreement/disagreement, sincerity/insincerity, and interest/boredom.

Often you are not fully aware of either sending or receiving messages in this way, but you can easily become more aware, and so improve your communication skills. The Body Language Vocabulary cards depict some of the main "words" or "phrases" used in body language.

Improving your language abilities

Just because your brain has lost its natural ability to learn simply by listening doesn't mean that learning new languages and developing your existing language abilities can't help your brain. Some research suggests that learning helps to maintain neurons in the state where they can still make many new connections, effectively keeping your brain young. Such "mental workouts" may be able to stave off age-related cognitive decline, and even Alzheimer's disease. Three strategies for maintaining and improving your language abilities are:

- Reading: Increases vocabulary and exposes you to challenging grammatical forms. The more advanced or difficult the reading matter, the better.

- Word games: Crosswords, acrostics (where the initial letters of words or lines in a piece make up a word themselves), and so on can all help with verbal abilities, as well as stimulating memory, problem solving, and creative thinking abilities.

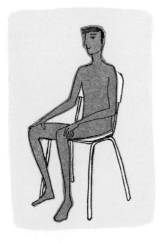

- Learning a language: This stimulates most parts of the intellect and has practical and social advantages, too.

Improving your nonverbal communication skills

Although most of us use body language in instinctive fashion, without being aware of it, you can train yourself to make better use of it, and to read other people's nonverbal messages more successfully. The first step is to develop awareness. Observing yourself in the mirror, or, even better, on

Goal checklist ✔

Language is a cognitive ability that is often taken too much for granted. Most people feel able to communicate at least adequately, and therefore don't feel an incentive to improve their language skills. However, if you practice the strategies and exercises outlined in the book and on these cards, you should be able to see some important improvements (listed over).

- ☐ Wider vocabulary, better spelling, and reduced frequency of errors in grammar
- ☐ More articulate speech
- ☐ Enhanced sensitivity to unspoken messages
- ☐ Ability to "read between the lines"
- ☐ Ability to anticipate and act early on requests/complaints
- ☐ Enhanced ability to speak without being interrupted, and to interrupt without causing offence
- ☐ Ability to make a better first impression

videotape, can provide surprising feedback on how you present yourself to others, in the same way that hearing your own voice on audiotape is often a shock. Making a habit of people-watching when you're out and about is a good way to become more aware of other people's body language. The Body Language Challenge cards give you specific guidelines on how to do this and what to look out for.

Go to page 140 for a series of exercises to test and improve your language and communication skills.

Hardware and Software

For most people memory is a psychological concept—a memory is something that exists in the mind, a product of thinking and feeling. In other words it is equivalent to something carried out by a piece of software, as though individual memories were processed by a program, in much the same way that a word-processing program deals with words. But just as software requires hardware in order to operate, so memory, like all mental functions, has its basis in the physical matter of the brain. If memory is software, the brain is hardware.

The memory trace

A memory is far more complex, however, than just two neurons swapping signals. Any one memory probably involves millions of neurons, connected in a circuit that has a particular pattern. Only if this circuit is activated in the correct pattern will that memory be triggered. If the same set of neurons were activated in even just a slightly different pattern, a completely different memory or other mental function might result.

How does this circuit, with its unique pattern, come to be formed? When you experience something, it causes an electrical signal to race through your brain, passing between millions of neurons, each of which triggers several others to fire off an electrical impulse. One theory is that it is this initial pattern of firing that is preserved as a memory—when the same pattern is reactivated, the experience is recalled.

This is where the analogy between brain and computer breaks down, as there is no longer a clear divide between hardware and software. The software equivalent—the memory "program"—takes the form of the pattern of neurons, which are the equivalent of hardware. This is why some writers call brain matter "wetware," to distinguish it from both hardware and software.

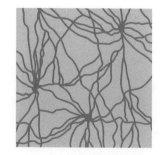

Memories in the brain

The brain is not simply a big ball of randomly connected neurons. It is organized into a complex structure, many different regions of which are involved in memory formation and storage.

Brainstem: The region where the spinal cord enters the skull and begins to swell into the brain is known as the brainstem, the topmost portion of which is called the midbrain. The brainstem controls basic, automatic functions such as breathing and blinking.

Thalamus: Sitting on top of the brainstem is a structure called the thalamus. This is the brain's information-processing and -integrating center, the first port of call for information arriving in the brain. The thalamus integrates information from different sources (such as the senses) and relays it to the appropriate structures in the rest of the brain. As the gateway for incoming information from the senses, the thalamus probably plays an important role in the workings of the sensory register.

Hippocampus: Named for its supposed resemblance to a seahorse, the hippocampus is part of the limbic system (see Memory mystery on page 39). It plays important roles in many different aspects of memory, such as training in new skills, learning new facts, and recognizing faces and places.

Amygdala: Attached to the end of the hippocampus is the amygdala, which is also part of the limbic system. This walnut-shaped structure plays an important role in the encoding stage of memory.

Cortex: Surrounding the brainstem and the limbic system is the main mass of the brain—the cerebrum. In the outer layer of the cerebrum, known as the cerebral cortex, neurons form dense networks of connections, and this is where memories are thought to be stored.

Distributed storage

Prior to the 1960s, it was assumed that specific memories must be represented in the brain by specific networks of neurons in specific parts of the cortex, so that it would effectively be possible to cut the physical trace of a memory out of the cortex and thus delete that memory. However, in the 1960s research was done on patients undergoing brain surgery. Each patient remained conscious during the operation while the surface of the brain (the cortex) was exposed. By stimulating the cortex with tiny electrodes, surgeons could trigger memories, but to their surprise they also found that the same memory could be triggered by stimulating widely different spots. From this work has developed the theory that the networks of neurons representing memories are not confined to one spot, but are distributed across the cortex and other parts of the brain.

Neural holograms

In 1969 Karl Pribram refined this theory with his neural hologram model. In a hologram the way that the original image is recorded is different from conventional photography. In a regular photograph each part of the photo records the equivalent part of the original image. So if you cut a photo into four quarters each quarter will depict only the matching quarter of the original image. In a hologram, however, every point on the hologram's surface contains a record of the entire original image. If you smash a hologram into pieces, each piece will depict all the original image (but with reduced clarity compared with the whole). Pribram suggested that memory is stored in the brain in a similar fashion to an image in a hologram, with a memory stored across a whole area of the brain. Any part of this area can be used to reconstruct the original memory, although we need to use the whole area to recall the memory with total clarity.

Infinite connectivity

There are more than 100 billion neurons in your brain, which means that the number of neuron-to-neuron interconnections is astronomical: around 100 trillion. There are more of these connections than there are leaves on all the trees in the Amazon rainforest.

Pribram's theory explains how losing function in parts of your brain (through aging or excessive drinking, for instance) can result in a degradation of memory rather than a total loss. It also accounts for why you sometimes remember scenes or episodes only vaguely, rather than remembering some parts of the scene not at all and other parts with full clarity. However, the opposite can also be true—you might remember virtually nothing about your first visit to the beach except for the taste of

Memory mystery:
Why are smells so evocative?

 The limbic system is a set of structures that sit between the midbrain and the cerebrum. We know that this system plays important roles in memory and emotion, although the details are poorly understood. Closely connected to the limbic system are the brain structures known as the olfactory bulbs, which gather and process information from the sense of smell. This information is relayed directly to the limbic system, giving the sense of smell a uniquely intimate connection to memory and emotion. This is why smells can trigger powerful emotional responses and also bring vivid and moving memories flooding back unexpectedly.

your first ice-cream cone, which you can recall with total clarity. So Pribram's theory is not necessarily the whole story.

Memory software

Having looked at the hardware, or rather "wetware," of the brain, let's now examine the software that runs on that wetware. One of the most important and influential models of memory is the modal model. According to the modal model, there are three primary types, or modes, of memory—the sensory register, short-term memory (also known as working memory), and long-term memory. The diagram overleaf shows the model, with the different modes and the processes that are involved in moving from one mode to the next.

Data feeds and flash memory: the sensory register

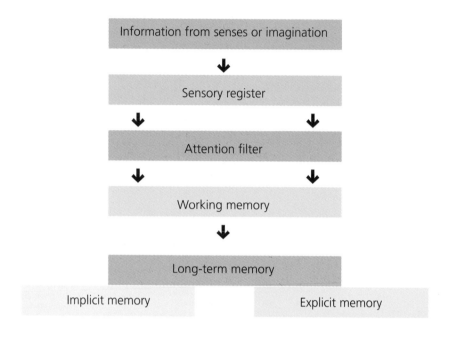

Before you can remember information, it must first arrive in your brain. Information from the outside world arrives via the senses, which feed the data they collect to the appropriate parts of your brain. When this information first arrives in the brain, it is held in a kind of mental clearing house known as the sensory register, which is the mental equivalent of flash memory in a computer.

Flood defences

Every millisecond of the day, information is flooding in from your senses. Your eyes, for instance, provide a series of incredibly detailed snapshots of whatever's in front of them. Most of this information, however, is not relevant or helpful to you, and there's no need to store it long enough even to become consciously aware of it. Quite the opposite, in fact—you need to erase it to avoid the risk of sensory overload. The job of the sensory register is to prevent sensory overload, while keeping hold of the sensory information in such a way that it can undergo the first stages of identification and analysis. An example of this is the process of pattern recognition, where the brain matches the sensory information to known patterns stored in the memory.

Pay attention

From the mass of information momentarily held in the sensory register, only a tiny fraction makes it to the next stage of memory—your short-term memory. The "raw" data is filtered by the mechanism of attention, and only those things you pay attention to are preserved. This is not to say that you consciously scan all the incoming sensory information and notice some parts. Much of the filtering must be unconscious.

The unconscious nature of this attention filter is easily demonstrated with the so-called cocktail-party effect, a phenomenon you have probably encountered yourself. At a cocktail party you may find yourself chatting to someone amid a hubbub of other conversations. Because your conscious attention is focused on the person you are chatting to, it seems as though you can't hear what the other guests are saying to one another. But if one of these other guests mentions your name in their conversation, you are likely to notice it. Evidently some part of your mind has been monitoring those other conversations. So it's a combination of the conscious and unconscious mechanisms of attention that helps to filter out most of the contents of the sensory register.

Persistence of vision

The existence of the sensory register, the most short-lived form of memory, is what makes cinema and television possible. They depend on a phenomenon called persistence of vision to create the illusion of continuous motion from a series of stills. Each frame of a movie or TV program is held as an icon in the visual register for a few milliseconds. By the time one icon is lost, the next frame has appeared and been processed into the register. If the frame rate of a film is slowed below a certain critical point, the images will be lost from the visual register more quickly than they are refreshed, and you start to notice a flickering, disjointed effect.

Icons and echoes

There are actually several different sensory registers—one for each sense. Research shows that each type has different storage properties, although all of them store memories for only brief periods. The visual register, for instance, stores images, technically known as icons, for less than half a second. The auditory register stores what are known as echoes for up to two seconds.

Malfunctions and Gremlins

If memory were perfect, there would be no need for you to be reading this book. There are, however, many flaws built into the natural working and development of the brain's everyday memory system.

Blocking

A common and irritating experience is the certainty that you know something but can't quite bring it to mind. When it involves words, this is known as the "tip-of-the-tongue" phenomenon, but it can also apply to other types of memory—e.g., not being able to think of the name of someone you know well, having a "mental block," or "going blank" about an essential piece of information that you normally recall without problem.

Somehow your memory is being blocked. Blocking can be caused by interference from another memory, such as when you can't think of the right answer to a question and can't stop bringing to mind an answer you know to be wrong. There are probably also other reasons—possibly neurological—that we simply don't understand.

Amnesia

The partial or complete loss of memory for recent or remote events or experiences is termed amnesia. Many types of disturbances or damage to the brain can cause it, and there are many kinds of amnesia. The best-known is the type that results from a blow to the head or from a stroke. This usually leads to immediate amnesia, where the person loses all memory of what happened immediately before the injury. It is caused by interruption of the process by which short-term memories (STM) are transferred to long-term storage. Since the information temporarily stored in STM is lost before it has been passed on for storage in more permanent form, it is irretrievable. Anything that causes loss of consciousness, such as a drinking binge, can also cause immediate amnesia.

A more severe injury or stroke may result in retrograde amnesia—amnesia for events in the past. How far back this stretches depends on the brain injury, but usually most of the memories are recovered over time.

A much rarer form is anterograde amnesia, the inability to form new long-term memories. This form of amnesia, today best-known from the film *Memento*, results from very specific damage to parts of the limbic system through injury or thiamine deficiency (usually linked to alcoholism). Anterograde amnesiacs retain their memories from before the damage occurred and can also form new procedural memories.

A more or less total loss of memory that only lasts between 30 minutes and 12 hours is known as transient global amnesia. Caused by a temporary blockage of the blood supply to the brain, it is usually associated with cardiovascular disease.

Amnesia may have psychological rather than physical causes. Mental breakdown or trauma, for instance, can cause dissociative amnesia. In this, areas of memory are mentally blocked off, or dissociated, and become inaccessible until the psychological problem is resolved. This type of amnesia usually affects only autobiographical memory, with the sufferer retaining semantic and procedural memory. For instance, a sufferer might remember who the U.S. President is and how to ride a bicycle or speak a foreign language, but not know his own name or whether he has a family. An extreme example of this dissociative amnesia is a condition known as fugue, where the sufferer leaves home and starts a new life in a new place with a new identity, apparently forgetting entirely about his or her old identity and past.

False memories and suggestibility

Memories of things that never happened, known as false memories, can be created in people through suggestion. Hypnosis produces a highly suggestible state, and this

Infantile amnesia

Everyone suffers from a form of amnesia known as infantile or childhood amnesia: the inability to remember events or experiences before the age of around three years. Some people claim to remember events preceding this but are probably constructing such memories from later information and experiences.

No one knows exactly why infantile amnesia exists but there are several theories. Some experts argue that an infant cannot form autobiographical memories because of a poorly developed sense of self. Others think that language is essential to autobiographical memory formation, and that until children master language properly they cannot form memories that their adult selves can understand. Another explanation is that children focus on what makes experiences similar, rather than the things that make them different (and therefore memorable).

is the main process by which false memories are formed. A classic example is someone who is hypnotized to recall past lives or alien-abduction experiences. However, hypnosis is not the only way that we form false memories. Memories of child abuse or even satanic-ritual abuse can be created by the suggestions of well-meaning social workers.

On a more mundane level, you can encourage false memories simply by asking leading questions. For instance, show a friend a picture of a car stopped at a "Stop" marking on the street, but with no street sign present. Later, ask them, "What did the street sign say?" They may be quite convinced that it said "Stop" and won't believe you when you tell them there was no sign.

Aging and memory

Memory problems are among the most obvious psychological symptoms of old age. Memory deteriorates with age for several reasons. One reason is that you lose brain cells throughout life from childhood onward—as many as 100,000 a day! Over the course of your life you can expect to lose about seven percent of the cells you had during childhood. In the overall scheme of things, however, this is not too bad.

A more serious factor is the change in your brain tissue as you age. Making new connections between brain cells becomes more difficult, and tangles of material can build up in the cortex, blocking and interfering with the normal brain functions. Psychological factors probably play a part in age-related memory problems. Some elderly people have restricted sensory environments and do not receive much mental stimulus, and this in turn may affect all of their mental abilities, memory included.

Remaining intellectually and socially active can counteract many age-related memory problems. Older people may find memory exercises such as those on the cards particularly useful, as simply making use of memory and testing its limits can help keep it in good working order.

Inside the brain: memory tangles

 Research by neurologists at Northwestern University in 2003 showed that age-related memory loss is associated with the buildup of tangled clumps of protein fragments inside nerve cells in the brain. They found that the number of these tangles, which may simply be a natural consequence of aging, related to the severity of memory loss. Very high levels of these tangles are known to be associated with Alzheimer's disease (although they should not be confused with the plaques of beta-amyloid protein that also occur in brains afflicted with Alzheimer's).

Exercises and strategies to try

Language booster

Help protect your mental powers against the effects of aging by learning a foreign language. It has long been suspected that this does work, but now there's scientific evidence to prove it. Researchers have used brain scans to show that people who speak a second language actually enlarge parts of their brains.

- The earlier you learn a second language, the more effect it has, but it is never too late to begin.
- Studying a foreign language will help improve your linguistic memory in general.
- If you already speak one foreign language, then maintain the brain workout by learning another.

Spelling cheats

Improve your spelling of hard-to-spell words with mnemonics like the following:

- To remember how many Cs and Ss there are in "necessary," a useful mnemonic is, "Only one 'C' is necessary to escape" ("two S-cape").
- To help you remember how to spell "rhythm" you could use the letters as an acronym—e.g., the first "R" might stand for "Rapid" while the final "M" might stand for "Madness."
- To help you remember the difference between "principal" and "principle," bear in mind that "your principal is your pal."

Tip-of-the-tongue finder

Here's how to overcome the frustration of something being "on the tip of your tongue":

- Say aloud any words that spring to mind instead of the one you are looking for. Such words often share characteristics, such as the same initial letter or the same number of syllables.
- Say out loud the meaning of the word you are searching for, describing it as fully as you can.
- Say any words you can think of with the same meaning.

Any of these approaches may serve as a cue for the correct word.

Familiar acrostics

Make uninteresting information memorable by using acrostics as mnemonic devices. An acrostic is a phrase, sentence, or verse made using words for which the initials are important in some way. Shown below are some relatively well-known acrostics.

- Acrostic for spelling "rhythm": Rhythm Helps Your Two Hips Move
- Order of taxonomy in biology (kingdom, phylum, class, order, family, genus, species): Kids Prefer Cheese Over Fried Green Spinach
- Order of the eight planets in the solar system: (Mercury, Venus, Earth, Mars, Jupiter, Saturn, Uranus, and Neptune): My Very Easy Method: Jet to the S U N
- Order of the colors of the rainbow (red, orange, yellow, green, blue, indigo, violet): Richard Of York Gave Battle In Vain
- Points of the compass running clockwise from the top (north, east, south, west): Never Eat Sweet Wheat
- Order in which notes fall on the treble clef (EGBDF): Every Good Boy Does Fine
- Attributes of living things in biology (nutrition, irritability, movement, growth, respiration, reproduction, excretion): Now I Must Go Right Round Europe
- Order in which mathematical operations are performed (multiply and divide before you add and subtract): My Dear Aunt Sally

Days in a month

Use one of these two mnemonics and you will never again wonder how many days there are in any given month.

- The month rhyme: 30 days hath September/ April, June, and November./ All the rest have 31/ Excepting February alone,/ Which hath but 28 in fine/ Till leap year gives it 29.
- The knuckle method: Make fists of both hands and hold them out in front of you with the thumbs inward. Put them together so that the thumbs are hidden. The knuckles stand for months with 31 days, the depressions for months with 30 (except February, of course, which usually has 28). Starting at the far left, the first knuckle is January, the first depression February, and so on.

Understanding IQ

IQ stands for intelligence quotient and is a measure of how intelligent you are. This begs a question that must be answered before we go any farther in exploring the meaning of IQ—what, precisely, do we mean by intelligence?

Defining IQ

Most people know intuitively what they mean when talking about intelligence, but struggle to come up with a consistent definition if asked to spell it out. The experts have the same problem—according to *Intelligence: Knowns and Unknowns*, a 1996 report from the American Psychological Association's Task Force on intelligence, "When two dozen prominent theorists were recently asked to define intelligence, they gave two dozen somewhat different definitions."

One definition, signed by 52 leading researchers in the field, states, "[Intelligence is] a very general mental capability that, among other things, involves the ability to reason, plan, solve problems, think abstractly, comprehend complex ideas, learn quickly, and learn from experience. It is not merely book learning, a narrow academic skill, or test-taking smarts. Rather, it reflects a broader and deeper capability for comprehending our surroundings—'catching on,' 'making sense' of things, or 'figuring out' what to do."

Although IQ is a measure of intelligence it is, in fact, a lot more specific than this. Specifically, your intelligence quotient is a measure of how intelligent you are for your age, in relation to the rest of the population, and is determined by your score on tests of your mental abilities. Modern IQ tests work by testing several different types of mental ability, such as your ability with words, your ability with numbers, or your ability to manipulate shapes in your mind's eye, and your scores on these tests are combined to give an overall score.

This score is then compared with the average score, and the calculation gives your IQ. Your IQ is therefore a way of describing your intelligence compared with other people (other adults, to be precise). This is one important reason why IQ tests are different from regular academic exams. By definition, an IQ of 100 is the average—

if you achieved a score of 100 on an IQ test, it would mean that you were of average intelligence for your age.

What IQ is not

What IQ is not can be as important as what it is in gaining a better handle on this much-misunderstood concept:

- IQ is not the same thing as intelligence, although the difference between the two things depends on whom you ask. Some psychologists argue that IQ tests only test very specific aspects of intelligence, and that an IQ score is a poor description of someone's overall intelligence because it misses out important aspects such as, for example, how good they are with people or how good they are with their hands. Others argue that IQ tests are an almost perfect measure of intelligence and that therefore someone's IQ score is an excellent description of their intelligence.

- IQ is not a measure of knowledge, wisdom, or memory, although these may well be related to your IQ score, just as they may be related to your intelligence. Memory in particular—or at least some types of memory—may play an important role in determining your performance on IQ tests.

- IQ is primarily a measure of performance. Your IQ score is a measure of how you performed on that test at that point. You may have the potential to perform much better.

There are two other important things you need to know about IQ:

- IQ scores are partly, but by no means entirely, determined by your genes—in other words you inherit some of your intelligence from your parents.

- IQ scores are associated with lots of other important things, such as academic achievement, earning power, and even health and life expectancy. This does not mean that a high IQ necessarily directly causes better health or better grades, but simply that the two seem to be linked in some way. This is pretty much what you'd expect, given that IQ is a measure of intelligence and intelligence plays a part in your ability to do everything from learning successfully to making good health choices. Remember that the word "correlates" can be misleading—for any individual, hard work, dedication, supportive parents, a good school or any of a hundred other variables could influence academic success or life achievements more than IQ.

IQ tests then and now

Since ancient times people have wondered about intelligence and what makes some people smarter than others. The first systematic attempt to compare intelligence (or at least some features of it) was in ancient China, where rigorous exams for the civil service selected the top 0.0001 percent of candidates based on their study of the philosopher Confucius. In the West, the first attempts to measure intelligence came in the late 19th century, but the history of IQ tests really begins in 1904 when the French psychologist Alfred Binet was commissioned by the government to devise a way to ensure that French children were being sent to the right schools.

Mental age vs. chronological age

Binet and his colleague Theodore Simon devised a rudimentary intelligence test for children, along with a scale of which scores were "normal" for which ages. This meant that an individual child's score could be used to describe their mental age, which might be different from their chronological age.

The Binet–Simon scale was later adapted by the American psychologist Lewis Terman, working at Stanford University, to give the Stanford–Binet test for adults. In devising the scoring system for his test, Terman wanted to come up with a way to express the scores that would allow comparison between people, so he included the concept of the intelligence quotient. By dividing a person's mental age (as determined by the test) by their chronological age, and then multiplying by 100 to give a nice round figure (which is easier to work with than decimals) he could compare different people.

Modern IQ tests

The Stanford–Binet scale has been developed and adapted over the years, but the same scoring principle of using a quotient has been retained, since it makes the results more meaningful. To be able to turn a person's score on a test into a quotient, it was necessary to standardize the tests by giving them to thousands of people and working out the average score, and the typical distribution of scores around that average. This information is then used to work out the IQ scores of individuals subsequently taking the test.

The early Stanford–Binet test mainly consisted of questions that tested a person's verbal abilities. However, it became obvious that it discriminated against people who were poorly educated, weren't native English speakers, or were simply more gifted in nonverbal abilities. This is why modern tests combine a variety of questions, to test a good spread of mental abilities.

What IQ tests really measure

If an IQ test is made up of different types of questions, which test different types of mental ability, how can it be used as a single measure? Aren't the different types of questions measuring different things? How can they be combined to give one overall score?

The common factor

It turns out that the different types of questions are probably measuring different aspects of the same thing, or at the very least that your ability in these different areas is due in large part to a single common factor. Psychologists reach this conclusion through a form of statistical analysis called regression analysis, which can work out how many factors are at work in determining scores in different tests, and whether common factors are involved.

How to interpret your IQ score

What most people really want to know when they find out their IQ score is what it means for them. An IQ score of 100, meaning that you are of exactly average intelligence, is the easiest to explain, but knowing how to interpret scores on either side of this mark is harder. The key concept to remember is that an IQ score is a way of expressing how you scored in relation to everyone else.

Percentiles

It is much more meaningful to express IQ as a percentile. An IQ score of 100 would put you in the 50th percentile, meaning that you had scored higher than 50 percent of people would if they took the test, but not as high as the other 50 percent. The table below shows what a particular IQ score means, in terms of percentile, for IQs of 74 and over. The table shows that 54 percent of the population scores between 89 and 111 (because 77 – 23 = 54).

IQ score distribution

IQ range	Percentile range
74 to 89	4–23
89 to 100	23–50
100 to 111	50–77
111 to 120	77–91
120 to 125	91–95
125 to 132	95–98
132 to 137	98–99.3
137 to 150	99.3–99.96
above 150	99.96–100

Components of IQ

If you look at the IQ test in this book you'll see that it consists of several different types of questions. There are questions featuring words and letters, questions featuring numbers and arithmetic, questions featuring shapes and patterns, and questions featuring sequences and progressions of all of these elements.

The purpose of having a range of question types is to test a range of mental abilities. Intelligence doesn't just consist of knowing how to use words or being able to perform speedy mental arithmetic. It has several different components.

Most intelligence tests look at four main components of intelligence by asking four different types of questions, all of which focus on ability rather than knowledge:

Verbal–linguistic: These test your ability with words and language, including comprehension and command of vocabulary.

Numerical–mathematical: These test your facility with numbers, including mental arithmetic and the ability to work out which mathematical operations you need to do to answer a question.

Visuospatial: These test your ability to work with shapes, patterns, and other visual material.

Logical: These test your ability to think logically, including identifying errors of reasoning.

Other types of abilities

The four types of mental abilities described obviously do not cover the whole field of human potential. There are several other types of abilities, such as creativity, wisdom, lateral thinking, and emotional intelligence (which is the term widely used to describe the ability to understand and deal with your own emotions, and with other people). These are all important in life, but they are also poorly understood and difficult to measure—two reasons why they are not generally included in IQ tests.

Are IQ tests for real?

IQ tests are controversial for lots of reasons, but one of the most critical charges leveled against them is that they do not deserve to be taken seriously, dismissed as having "nothing to do with the real world" or derided on the basis that they test only the ability to do well in IQ tests.

Is this fair? Do IQ tests really only test your ability to take IQ tests, or does your performance on them relate to important things in the real world? Are they a good measure of intelligence, or do they look at such a narrow range of abilities that they are effectively useless?

How many intelligences are there?

We've already seen how, despite the fact that IQ tests break down into four subtypes of questions that test four subtypes of mental abilities, statistical analysis suggests that one underlying ability—named general intelligence, or g—determines your score. For many psychologists this is tantamount to proof that there is one overarching form of intelligence. But not everyone agrees, and there are several theories that say there are multiple types of intelligence, some or most of which are not properly tested by IQ tests.

The American psychologist Howard Gardner felt that the conventional theory of intelligence misses out several equally important types of intelligence, though some are similar to the types of mental abilities already included:

Verbal–linguistic: Similar to the ability tested by verbal–linguistic IQ
 questions, this intelligence involves words and language.

Fluid vs. crystallized intelligence

In the 1960s the American psychologist Raymond Cattell, among others, suggested that intelligence should be classified as either fluid or crystallized.

- Fluid intelligence is closer to what is commonly thought of as "raw" or "pure" intelligence and refers to abilities involving reasoning, abstract thought, and mental agility but doesn't depend on knowledge, information, experience, training, or education.

- Crystallized intelligence, on the other hand, is all about knowledge—about how the products of intelligent thought have "crystallized" into information and skills. It includes vocabulary, general knowledge, knowing shortcuts or how to do things, and the fruits of experience.

Logical–mathematical: This is similar to a combination of the logical and the numerical–mathematical abilities already described.

Visuospatial: Similar to the visuospatial ability described above.

Body–kinesthetic: This involves muscular coordination, movement, and balance.

Auditory–musical: Hearing and the understanding of sound, particularly music—such as being good at hearing pitch or following rhythms.

Intrapersonal: Understanding and dealing with your own thoughts and feelings.

Interpersonal: This involves understanding, dealing with, and communicating with other people.

Naturalist: Understanding and working with natural things and systems and with the environment.

Stick with g

Most psychologists, though, are sceptical about Gardner's theory, and while they accept that there are different subtypes of intelligence, they also point to the evidence and the statistics. These seem to show that there really is one underlying form of intelligence—g—and that Gardner's intelligences are strongly related to it. In other words, people with a high g are more likely to be wise and creative, and have both fluid and crystallized intelligence. Since IQ tests are known to be a good way of measuring g, it seems that they really do measure intelligence in a meaningful way.

IQ tests and the real world

Perhaps the most common folk-wisdom objection to IQ testing is that the results have little or nothing to do with real life, and that all the braininess in the world won't help you to graduate from the school of hard knocks. And on the surface the talent of predicting whether the next shape in a series should be a triangle inside a hexagon doesn't seem to bear much relation to real-world tasks.

The evidence, however, very clearly shows that performance on IQ tests does have a lot of relevance to real-world issues, and in particular that it is a good predictor of everything from educational attainment and career success to wealth and health. For example, it has been shown that people with high IQ scores are more likely to do better at school, get better and more highly paid jobs and be more successful at them, and

live longer and stay healthier later in life than people with low IQ scores. Studies on the use of IQ-style testing as a tool for selecting job applicants show that it is as good at choosing successful employees as detailed, structured interviews and better than other measures such as years of job experience.

When it comes to individuals, the case is less clear, because for any individual other factors can prove much more important. These range from upbringing and childhood environment to personal motivation and conscientiousness. For example, someone who scores poorly on IQ tests but is hardworking and perseveres can easily outperform a super-intelligent slacker.

Is IQ set at birth?

It is generally accepted that we inherit a lot from our parents but most people would like to believe that intelligence is not fixed at birth, so that even if a child has parents who are not very intelligent, the child could overcome any intellectual limitations given the right opportunities. The way a child is brought up is also thought to be vitally important to intellectual development, and that, for instance, bringing up a child in a supportive, stimulating environment would help the child to become more intelligent than if they were neglected.

Tales of twins and adoptees

Testing these predictions is quite difficult, because most children get both their genes and their upbringing from their parents, which makes it impossible to tell which factor has the greater influence on IQ. Social "experiments" involving identical twins and children who are adopted show that, on average, family upbringing has very little influence on eventual IQ (the IQ that someone has as an adult). You can take a child away from their biological parents and have them raised by another family alongside

their children, but no matter how good or bad the childhood environment that this family provides, it will have very little effect on the child's IQ as an adult.

This is a surprising and, for many, disturbing finding. It does not mean that your IQ is entirely determined by your genes, because the studies also show that environmental factors in general do have a strong effect on IQ, but genes are a very strong influence. On average, 50 percent of the difference between the IQ scores of any two people comes down to the genetic differences between them. So if you're a near-genius and the person sitting next to you is a dunce, that's around 50 percent due to the difference between your genes, and 50 percent to your different life experiences.

The Flynn effect

In 1984, James Flynn, a political scientist at the University of Otago in New Zealand, published the first of a series of papers drawing attention to a strange trend that had previously gone unnoticed. The companies that made and sold IQ tests were having continually to revise their scoring systems to maintain an average IQ of 100, because people seemed to be scoring better in IQ tests each year. Flynn discovered that in order to get the same IQ today as someone who did the identical test 20 years earlier, you would have to perform much better. Or, to put it another way, if you got the exact same score on the exact same test, but 20 years apart, you would be awarded a significantly lower IQ score in the modern day.

The reason for this continual revision of the scoring system was that the average performance seemed to be getting better year on year. Flynn discovered that, on average, people in the developed world were gaining about half an IQ point per year, or about 15 IQ points over 30 years. If you went back to 1945 and used today's scoring standards (which are based on today's average performances), you would find that the average IQ was around 70, which is borderline mentally disabled.

These amazing findings seem to suggest that either most people in the 1940s were mentally subnormal or most people today are highly intelligent, but common sense tells us this is not the case. We have not seen a radical boost in the number of geniuses or in general intellectual attainment, while many people argue that educational standards have fallen and that attainment is lower than in the past.

One suggested explanation is that improved diet and healthcare have led to better brains. Another is that people have become increasingly familiar with IQ-type questions. A third explanation is that Flynn got his arithmetic wrong. The evidence supports none of these explanations, however. The Flynn effect is real, but it remains a mystery.

Can IQ be improved?

The evidence from these studies of twins and adoptees suggests that by adulthood people will end up with a given IQ no matter what environment they are raised in. This suggests that you are stuck with the IQ you were born with, in much the same way as you are basically stuck with your height once you are fully grown, and all the exercise or diets in the world won't change it. Remember, however, that IQ is a measure of performance, and there are plenty of things you can do to improve your performance on IQ tests.

Turn to page 144 to find a full IQ test to see how you fare.

Part Two

How You Remember

Memory and Concentration

Memory consists of several different systems that work together to help form, store, and retrieve information and experiences. The different systems allow us to sort through the flood of information supplied by our senses and select the important stuff to be laid down as memories. In this chapter we'll look at how this process works, and how you can use that knowledge to improve your memory.

Memories in the brain

What do memories look like? If you could look at the brain under a microscope, would you be able to point to a specific structure that represents a memory? In fact, memories do not exist as simple structures, but as networks. A single memory is composed of a circuit of neurons (nerve cells) that fire in a particular pattern. Anything that sets off one of the neurons in the circuit could trigger that memory, although a different pattern of firing, involving the same circuit of neurons, could trigger a different memory.

Types of memory

According to one theory, there are three main types of memory—the sensory register, short-term memory (also known as working memory), and long-term memory.

The sensory register

Information from the sense organs and from other parts of the brain (e.g., your imagination) is held briefly in a very short-term form of memory known as the sensory register. You are not consciously aware of everything held here (there's just too much information to take in at this stage). The mechanism of attention selects information that is important or striking in some way, so that you become consciously aware of it. The rest of the sensory register contents are filtered out and lost before you even knew they were there.

Using your senses to focus attention

Attention is what determines whether you notice and retain information. Events that grab your attention tend to be very memorable. Things that you don't pay proper attention to are likely to be forgotten. You can use your senses to enhance your attentiveness and memory. Make a conscious effort to focus completely on whatever you are doing, taking notice of all the different sensory aspects of the situation. If you are eating a meal, for instance, pay close attention to the tastes, smells, and textures, to the shape and color of the food, and to the sounds around you at the time.

Engaging all of your senses like this will automatically improve your memory, and the more you practice it, the more naturally it will come.

Short-term memory

Short-term memory (STM) is where you hold information that you need to use in the here and now. It is sometimes described as a "mental workplace" and this practical aspect is reflected in its alternative name, working memory. The classic example of STM in action is when someone tells you a phone number that you need to dial. The sequence of numbers is held in your memory just long enough for you to use it. Your STM is also essential for functions such as reading, planning, and writing messages, and doing mental arithmetic.

Information stored in the STM has a limited lifespan; unless it is rehearsed (i.e., unless you mentally repeat the information to yourself, going over it in your mind) it will fade away, or decay, within a few seconds. Rehearsal, decay, and a related phenomenon called interference are explored in more detail on page 61.

STM as RAM

A good analogy for STM is the type of computer memory called Random Access Memory (RAM). This is the part of a computer system that loads information from a permanent store, or gets it from the ongoing processes of the computer, and holds it for a short while so that other computer components and programs can use it. Because this cache of information needs to be changed frequently, RAM only stores it temporarily. If you turn off the computer, all the data in RAM is lost. The same thing happens with a person—if someone is knocked unconscious, all the information stored in their STM will be lost, which is why people who are knocked out usually have no memory of what happened to them immediately beforehand.

Types of STM

Experiments on how much people can remember over short periods of time show that they can store more if the information comes in different formats (e.g., lists of words together with series of images, rather than simply two lists of words). This suggests that there are actually several different types or sub-systems of STM. The most important ones seem to be an STM for visual imagery and one for verbal or audio information.

The STM for visual imagery is called the visuospatial sketchpad. This is similar to a wipe-clean whiteboard. Images or mental maps are stored here while other functions, such as forward planning, are carried out using the information.

The best understood sub-system of STM is the phonological loop, which stores units of auditory information. Usually this means the syllables that make up speech, but it also includes numbers or simply noises. Research shows that the phonological loop itself has two components. One is a phonological store, where about two-seconds' worth of information is held; the other is a rehearsal device, where you repeat the information in the store in a loop, but without actually saying the words or noises. This constantly refreshes the information held in the store so that it remains accurate, which is important for the proper functioning of language abilities, such as associating sounds with meanings and learning new words.

In addition to the visuospatial sketchpad and the phonological loop, evidence suggests that there may also be distinct STM sub-systems for meaning, odors, and, in deaf people, sign language.

Miller's magic number

During the 1950s, research by Harvard psychologist George Miller demonstrated that the average capacity of STM—the number of bits or chunks of information it can hold—is seven. This has become known as Miller's magic number, although he himself usually describes it as seven plus or minus two, because of the variation between individuals. In other words some people can remember nine items of information in the short term, and others only five.

What this means is that, given lists of numbers, names, or letters to look at and then recite back, most people can recite a list of seven items before some of the items are forgotten. You can try this for yourself with the digit-span test on page

Memory mystery:
Why can't I get that jingle out of my head?

Sometimes when you want to forget something, you find that you can't. When it is an irritating tune from an ad jingle or the latest tinny pop hit, it can drive you to distraction. Often these tunes are designed to be memorable, and when one is stuck in your head it means that it has succeeded in latching on to your phonological loop. Because this sub-system of your STM is designed to rehearse sounds in a constant loop so that they don't fade through decay, it can have the effect of a broken record. The best way to overcome the phenomenon is through distraction. If you can distract your attention from the tune for a few seconds, the phonological loop will stop rehearsing it long enough for it to fade away through the natural process of decay.

160, which looks at your short-term capacity for numbers, or "digit span." The items that your STM works with are not simply numbers. The magic number can apply to words, concepts, images, noises, musical notes—anything that comes as a discrete "package" of information. This fact is the basis of a memory-boosting method named chunking (see page 62), where you reorganize information that you need to remember into chunks, and use the title or label of each chunk as a cue to remember the rest of it.

Miller's research had far-reaching consequences for telecommunications. Telephone companies, worried that customers would not want long numbers, made sure that telephone numbers consisted of no more than seven digits (with added prefix codes). Similarly, in today's cellphone age, most people's numbers consist of an initial code common to other cellphone numbers, followed by a unique series of only six numbers, in line with Miller's principle.

Decay and interference

Because the STM is used for moment-to-moment tasks, it wouldn't pay to have it clogged up with too many items held for too long. Fast decision-making on the hoof, which is what STM is for, requires that only the minimum amount of information is held in working memory at any one time. This is why STM has a limited capacity. The processes that limit that capacity are decay and interference. Decay is where memories fade away naturally when they are not rehearsed. Interference is where the arrival of new items of information in the STM pushes out existing items. To see decay and interference working in practice, look at the exercises on page 160.

Chunking

To make it easier to remember long lists, organize the information into chunks, as explained overleaf. Chunking helps with short-term memory, because instead of remembering only, say, seven small pieces of information, you can remember seven large chunks of information. It also helps improve long-term memory, because if you organize the chunks around some internal logic, you can recall several things by calling to mind a single chunk.

- Break a long number down into smaller numbers, with two to four digits each—if possible, ones that are memorable, such as years or personally significant dates.

- Organize larger amounts of information into seven chunks, each with a heading, and then memorize the headings.

A good analogy for the processes is to think of the STM as being like someone spinning plates. If the plate-spinner doesn't go back to each plate to give it another spin (rehearsal), it will spin more and more slowly until it falls over and is lost—this is like decay. If the plate-spinner tries to spin more than his maximum of seven plates, he won't be able to keep them all up—this is equivalent to the maximum capacity of STM. If new plates are added to the lineup and he has to keep them spinning, some of them will be lost—equivalent to interference.

Long-term memory

For our purposes the most important stage in the memory process is the transition from short-term to long-term memory. This stage, known as encoding, determines whether a memory will be stored for the long-term or will simply fade away and be lost for ever. Encoding affects how long and how securely the memory will be stored, in what form it will be stored, how easy it will be to recall at a later date, and even the way in which later recall will work.

Types of long-term memories

Not all LTMs are the same. Memories that you can consciously recall are known as explicit memories. Explicit memory includes memory for facts, names, places, etc., which is known as semantic memory. But there is also a type of memory that is not available to your conscious awareness. This is called implicit memory, and includes learned abilities (e.g., riding a bicycle) and things that you don't know you know—for instance, you might think someone looks familiar, but not know why. Your memory of having seen them before is implicit.

Attention and rehearsal

The first issue is the question of why some memories make it to the next stage and some don't. Attention and rehearsal, two of the processes that are important for short-term memory (STM), are involved here. STM items that are significant or noticeable in some way, such as information that is interesting, important, or emotionally charged, will catch and hold your attention. When your attention is focused on such information, it is held in your STM through the process of rehearsal, where the temporary information cache is refreshed constantly to stop information from fading away. If you keep this up for long enough, the process of transferral to longer-term storage gets underway.

Encoding memories

In order to become part of the brain's long-term memory store, a memory must be encoded, that is, recorded as a set of memory elements that can later be reassembled to recover the memory. Encoding is not simply a one-step process. Instead there are different levels of encoding, corresponding to particular levels of storage. Initial encoding of a memory shifts it to a kind of intermediate memory store, where it may last for anywhere from an hour to a few days. If the information is revisited in some way—i.e., it is used, or brought to mind, or the original stimulus that caused the memory is revisited—further encoding may lead to longer lasting storage.

So what happens when a memory is encoded? Memories are not like photographs, stored as snapshots that are complete in themselves. Rather, they are stored as a network of associations between the different elements of that particular memory.

A memory of your grandmother, for instance, would actually be composed of many different elements, including concepts of age, femininity, and maternity; sensory elements such as form, scent, and color; emotional elements such as fondness or love; and semantic (fact-based) elements, such as a name or location. Any of these elements is also associated with thousands, perhaps millions, of other memories, but a specific combination of them adds up to the memory of your grandmother.

The encoding process that laid down this memory involved building a new and unique network of associations between bits of information already stored in your brain, perhaps with the addition of a few new ones. (For example, when you first met your grandmother, her perfume may have been one you'd never encountered previously, or she was wearing a distinctive coat, giving you a series of new sensory experiences to store.)

Shallow and deep encoding

Not all encoding is equally effective. Encoding involves making connections between the elements of the memory and other memories and memory elements already present in the brain. If few such connections are made, the encoding is said to be shallow. Shallow encoding is what happens when you try to learn something in isolation—perhaps by simply repeating it to yourself—without considering it in a wider context or understanding it properly so that you can see how it connects to other knowledge or memories. Shallow encoding is fine when you need to remember things only for a little while, but it means that memories are less securely stored and will be more difficult to recall.

Deep encoding, by contrast, is where you form many strong connections between the new memory and existing ones. So, for instance, you are more likely to remember a day at the beach if it reminds you of childhood vacations or if it is a particularly romantic day (which then ties it in with a whole host of other associations to do with love and relationships). You are more likely to remember a mathematical equation if you understand how it was derived in the first place. In these cases the memory has been deeply encoded either because of powerful associations or because a thorough understanding involves drawing connections. Deeply encoded memories are more securely stored and easier to recall.

Memory mystery:
Why is it that my partner can remember every member of the 1987 championship winning team, but forgets the names of his nieces?

This is a common complaint, usually directed at men by women. There is probably more at work here than simple memory issues, however. Psychologists now believe that people vary not just in IQ but also in terms of "emotional intelligence," and that there is a spectrum of emotional intelligence, with highly empathetic people at one end and the autistic at the other extreme. People who fall toward the lower end of the spectrum may display a form of emotional incompetence sometimes known as Asperger's Syndrome, which is much more common in men than women. This may explain why some men don't seem to encode emotionally significant information as strongly as they ought to. Because of the way such a man's brain is set up, his amygdala labels information like a niece's name as unimportant compared with, say, seemingly trivial sporting information.

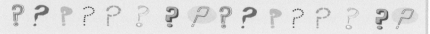

Inside the brain:
The labeling of memories

Stuck on the end of the limbic system is a walnut-shaped structure called the amygdala. Brain scans show that this structure plays a vital role in the formation of memories, because it is active when emotional memories are being formed. Experts believe that the amygdala is a kind of labeling device, which attaches emotional associations to a memory. For instance, if you are walking down a street and get a shock when a dog jumps out at you, it is the amygdala that attaches the emotional associations of fear and surprise to the memory of the incident. Because your "dog attack" memory has been thus labeled by the amygdala, recalling the dog will also bring back some of the emotion you felt at the time.

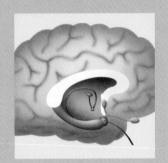

Pushing out the limits

Fascinating evidence for the potential capacity of human memory is provided by cases of extraordinary individuals. Some people claim to have a photographic memory (technically known as eidetic memory), where they have only to see an image once to be able to call it to mind as if it were actually in front of them. This suggests they are storing far more information than most people would have believed possible.

For the average person, forgetting is an essential process. It would be difficult to function if you recalled all information equally well—if you remembered, say, the distribution of drops of water on the windshield of your car from the morning of January 12, 1987, as well as you remembered the names of your loved ones or the time of your next meeting. We need to limit the amount of information in our minds if we are to process it efficiently.

It is impossible to put an absolute limit on the memory capacity of the human brain, but it is safe to say that almost everyone can remember more than they think, and that access to those memories can be improved by practicing the techniques outlined in this book.

Declarative memory

Psychologists draw a distinction between two types of long-term memory, known as declarative (or explicit) memory and procedural (or implicit) memory. Sometimes described as "knowing that," declarative memory is for things you know that you know, such as facts, people's names, where you went on vacation, how much a loaf of bread costs, or where your keys are. It breaks down further, into semantic and episodic memory.

Semantic memory: This is memory for facts and figures, names and words, the ability to recognize objects and animals—memory linked to meaning. Semantic memory is essential because it allows us to make sense of the world and to understand language.

Episodic memory: Memory for "episodes," or things that have happened, such as events, scenarios, or situations, is known as episodic memory. It includes autobiographical memory, which is memory for things that have happened to you, and is essential for your sense of identity. In stories and movies about amnesiacs, it is usually autobiographical memory that is missing, raising fascinating questions about identity and personality. If you don't have a past, are you really you? Would you still have a personality if all the history that had gone into shaping that personality were lost? A common theme in such situations is that the amnesiac feels that he is a decent person but discovers that he has done many bad things. Could that really happen?

Procedural memory

Sometimes described as "knowing how," procedural memory is the memory for skills, abilities, or procedures—things you do without really remembering how, such as walking, riding a bicycle, brushing your teeth, working a computer, or using money. It seems to be a separate system from declarative memory, as amnesiacs who lose their declarative memory often retain the procedural variety. Those amnesiacs who lose the ability to form new declarative memories—known as anterograde amnesiacs—can still learn new skills, even if they can't recall having done so.

Beyond comprehension

The most extreme example of photographic memory is that of a Russian known as "S," reported by the Russian psychologist Luria in the 1920s. "S" could apparently remember every single thing that had ever happened to him—every word of every conversation, every detail of every scene. But his comprehension of this material was very limited. It's hard to know what to make of this case. Should we take it literally? How could "S" (who had a job as a newspaper reporter) have functioned normally?

Memory mystery:
What is the storage capacity of the human brain?

If human memory were similar to data storage in a computer, the brain should have a maximum capacity for memory storage. However, memories are not stored in the same way as digital data, but through the interaction of networks of neurons and the patterns of firing in those networks. These networks and their patterns of connections can change over time, and so can memories, which are themselves composed of networks of associations.

It is hard to assess the extent of something so mercurial. What we can say is that, given the number of neurons in the brain, and the number of synapses between these neurons, the total number of theoretically possible connections between neurons is greater than the number of atoms in the universe. Perhaps the number of memories it is theoretically possible to have is similarly astronomical.

Exercises and strategies to try

Poems to boost memory

To practice your memorization skills and enhance your memory, learn some poems by heart. Here are two on the topic of memory.

One had a lovely face,
And two or three had charm,
But charm and face were in
  vain
Because the mountain grass
Cannot but keep the form.

"Memory," W. B. Yeats

To flee from memory
Had we the Wings
Many would fly
Inured to slower things
Birds with surprise
Would scan the cowering Van
Of men escaping
From the mind of man.
To flee from memory

Emily Dickinson

Quotes to boost memory

Memorizing quotations not only exercises your memory but also provides impressive conversation. Use these to boost your brain and inspire you:

- "God gave us memory so that we might have roses in December." J. M. Barrie
- "What we learn with pleasure we never forget." Alfred Mercier
- "There is not any memory with less satisfaction than the memory of some temptation we resisted." J. Branch Cabell
- "Nothing fixes a thing so intensely in the memory as the wish to forget it." Michel de Montaigne
- "Son, always tell the truth. Then you'll never have to remember what you said the last time." Sam Rayburn

Novel memories

If you find that you can't remember much about books you've read, it doesn't mean that you are memory-impaired—you just need to learn to read proactively. Here are some guidelines:

- If the book is factual, write down a list of questions and topics you expect it to address, before you read it.
- Go back to your list at intervals to see if your questions have been answered.
- Note down major plot points, characters, and passages in the margin or on a separate piece of paper as you read.
- After each chapter, review the contents by jotting down a list of salient points.
- At key stages in the book, use spider diagrams (see Card 67) to review your memory of plot and relationships.

Devise puns

Puns are the key element of many mnemonic strategies. Use them wherever possible to form associations. Because they are humorous, puns are encoded well and are thus easy to recall. For instance, if you want to remember that the name of Karen's partner is Harry, you might play on the fact that Karen is somewhat hirsute and pronounce Harry as "Hairy."

Memory Retrieval

In order for a memory to be of any use—in fact, for it to be a memory at all, rather than a pattern of neuronal connections lost in the tangle of your brain—it must be accessed and retrieved, brought to mind, or recalled.

It is tempting to imagine a memory as a particular circuit of neurons, forged by the original experience, where sending an electrical impulse around this circuit in the same pattern as the original stimulus recreates the experience. However, evidence shows that recall is a much more complicated process than this. Memories are not simply little computer routines, which can be run again and again, producing the exact same response each time. Nor are they like photographic negatives, which can be exposed over and over to produce an identical picture each time.

Reconstruction

A memory is a mental experience in the present that is constructed from elements that refer to the past. For instance, your memory of eating ice cream is built up from mental representations of such qualities as sweetness and coldness. In other words a memory is a reconstruction of the original experience. Remembering an experience is a bit like having a virtual experience that has been constructed to seem like the original. This explains why memory can be notoriously unreliable, and how different people can remember the same thing very differently. It is even possible to make people remember things that never actually happened to them.

Access made easy

The ease with which you can access a memory depends on how well it was encoded in the first place. High-quality encoding ensures that a memory is laid down as part of a rich network of associations. When it comes to recall, a memory is accessed via one or more of these associations.

For instance, if you are trying to remember that the capital of Nigeria is Abuja, you might come at the answer via your memory of having been there on holiday, via your knowledge of the provinces of Nigeria, or via a phonetic association you have formed between the word "Abuja" and the word "Nigeria."

The more associations that exist in your memory store, the greater the number of angles from which you can access this memory, and the easier it will be to recall. This is why good encoding is the key to successful recall.

Context counts
Research shows that one of the best ways to make it easier to access a memory is to recreate the context in which it was committed to memory. The original experiment that demonstrated this involved scuba divers who memorized material while under water. A few days later they were tested both underwater and on dry land and showed much better recall when under water. Recreating the initial learning context made recall much easier. This is the rationale for police reconstructions.

Similar effects can be shown in more mundane ways. If you learn a word in association with a second, unrelated word, your recall for the first word will be much better when the second word is again present. On a practical level, this can be used for recalling difficult-to-access memories or remembering where you left something.

Visualization and association
Visual imagery is the most memorable form of information. You can enhance your memory by visualizing things you need to remember. If items do not lend themselves automatically to visualization, associate them with something that does. Association increases the number of connections between memories and makes them easier to recall. Combining the two methods, by building up combinations of striking imagery

Memory mystery:
How is it possible that I remembered a particular experience as having happened to me, only to discover that it was actually a scene from a film?

This is a common experience, called misattribution, and reflects the reconstructive nature of memory. First you saw the film and committed the scene to memory. On recalling the scene, the reconstruction mechanism has left out the part about its being a movie, and substituted a personal point of view into the proceedings. Thus the memory becomes one involving you as a direct participant in the experience. The same thing can happen with scenes from books, stories told by other people, or scenes that are altogether imaginary and never happened to anyone. Memory can be very unreliable.

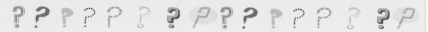

and arresting associations, is a great way to maximize your memory powers. The more bizarre and striking the imagery you use, the better—strange or humorous juxtapositions are particularly effective.

Music and memory

Research at the University of California at Irvine in the 1990s suggested that listening to classical music could enhance the intelligence of children, prompting a flurry of interest and massive sales of Mozart's Sonata for Two Pianos in D Major. Subsequent research has more or less debunked the Mozart Effect, but has shown that musical training, rather than simply listening to music, does boost memory power. There is also plenty of anecdotal evidence to suggest that soothing, structured music, like that by Mozart or Bach, can increase concentration levels, which in turn makes for more effective encoding and therefore recall.

Memory Lane

A classic strategy for combining visualization and association is to make up a story around items that you want to remember. This narrative can take any form, so long as the images and associations involved are suitably striking and memorable. A typical example is to imagine items that need to be memorized as being placed along a route of some sort. Recalling the list involves mentally traveling this imaginary path.

For instance, suppose you want to memorize the kings and queens of England. Starting at the Norman Conquest, the first three kings are William the Conqueror, William Rufus, and Henry I. An imaginary journey might start in the garden, with you looking at a bird holding a conker in its bill (Bill = William; conker = Conqueror); which it then drops in order to pick up a piece of rhubarb (Bill = William again; rhubarb = Rufus); before being chased off by a hairy dog (Hairy = Henry). The next king was Stephen—you could continue your mental journey by "stepping in" to the kitchen; and so on.

Go to pages 160–63 for a series of exercises to test and improve the different areas of your memory.

Exercises and strategies to try

Overcoming interference

How many times have you walked into a room to get something, only to
realize that you've forgotten what it was? How many times have you gone
out intending to do something during the day, only to arrive home later and
notice that you forgot to do it? Phenomena such as these are due to
interference—the process where new information arriving in your short-
term memory, with its limited capacity, pushes out old information.

You can overcome interference by making the original information more
memorable—use the visual association method, and transform the dry and
forgettable original info into a striking image that will stay with you, and
can be easily triggered by association. For instance, if you need to
remember to buy stamps next time you go out, imagine yourself being
stamped on by a giant foot if you return home without them. Visualize the
giant foot wearing something associated with a place you know you'll be
passing.

The knowledge

Cab drivers in London, England, have to pass a test of their geographical
prowess, known as "the Knowledge." In the test they have to describe
exactly, without cues or prompts of any kind, the fastest route between any
two points in the city. Some research suggests that training for the
Knowledge actually enlarges parts of the brain. You may not be able to
achieve this level of proficiency, but with practice you can radically improve
your memory of the street layout in your area.

- When out and about, get into the habit of visualizing your route as if
  you were looking at it on a map.

- Memorize routes from place to place by visualizing them in relation to
  main streets and landmarks that you already know.

- Use landmarks along main routes as triggers to recall lesser routes.

- Mentally practice difficult route-finding, and test yourself frequently.

Friends and their jobs

One of the most common memory complaints is difficulty remembering names, faces, and associated personal information. Such information is stored in your long-term memory. Quantify how good (or bad) your long-term memory is by constructing a flowchart of friends and friends of friends, and trying to fill in the details. Start off with a large blank piece of paper and draw a circle in the middle representing you. Then draw lines out to a ring of circles representing your closest friends and family. In each of the circles record the name and occupation of the person, and whether or not you remember his or her face.

Now try and draw a further layer of circles representing friends of your friends—people you've been introduced to and ought to remember. See how far out you can go, and for how many people you can accurately recall their name, occupation, and appearance. Try this exercise again in a few months, after you've incorporated memory-boosting strategies into your life, and compare the results to your initial effort. With enhanced powers of recall, the ring of people you can remember should widen.

Learn the rule of five

The rule of five says that repeating a fact five times fixes it in your memory, using repetitions at progressively longer intervals. Use this to memorize material for a speech or an essay.

Step 1: Break information down into five key points—headings you can use to cue the rest of the info. Record these headings in a list.

Step 2: Put this card and the list where you will see it daily, and time the repetitions in the Time point schedule below. When you come to repeat the info, first try to recall the points without looking at them.

Step 3: Now repeat the information you recorded on the list. Read the points out loud.

Step 4: By the time you reach "Time point 5", you should be able to recall the key points.

Time point schedule:

Time point 1: 1 hour Time point 2: 1 day Time point 3: 1 week Time point 4: 2 weeks Time point 5: 1 month

Remembering names

Forgetting people's names, almost as soon as you've been told them, is a common problem. Once again, this is due to the process of interference affecting short-term memory. Use the association method to fix a name in your memory. You can also try to fit the association to the person's appearance. Here are some common name-association examples:

- John: Long John Silver or John F. Kennedy
- Jane: Jane Fonda or Jane Austen
- Michael: Michael J. Fox or Michael Douglas
- Katherine: Catherine the Great or Catherine Zeta Douglas
- Steven: Steve Tyler or Steven Spielberg
- Lucy: Lucy in the Sky with Diamonds or Lucy Liu
- Emily: Emily Post or Emily Dickinson

Goal checklist ✔

Memory is a faculty that can be radically improved by practicing the strategies and exercises outlined in the book and on these cards. Use the self-assessment tests and exercises, such as Kim's game and the digit-span test, at regular intervals to check your progress. In a few weeks you should see improvements such as:

☐ Proficiency at recalling names and details of people you meet, and places you visit

☐ Proficiency at rapidly forming associations and visualizations

☐ Better recall of events in your recent history (e.g., what you did last Thursday night)

☐ Better recall of facts and figures

☐ Better recall of details of books read, and movies and TV shows watched

Troubleshooter: Memory Problem Solver

Most people become aware of their memory only when it causes them problems, with varying degrees of inconvenience and distress. Trivial lapses can be shrugged off, particularly when the cause is obvious—for instance, if you were distracted, if something important happened to interrupt you, or if you knew at the time that the item to be remembered was too minor or boring. But memory lapses can also be embarrassing, upsetting, or even harmful. Forgetting someone's name can seem like an insult. Leaving something important behind can be a nuisance and can easily cause anxiety in older people, who may be acutely conscious of memory failings. Forgetting to do something at work could impair your career.

Do not despair, however, for help is at hand. This section covers some of the most common, important, and exasperating types of memory problems. It explains the underlying causes and examines how understanding these causes leads to useful solutions, ranging from quick tips and handy hints to new ways of interacting with the world that can permanently improve your memory abilities.

Memory for names and faces

One of the most common problem areas in memory is the issue of remembering names and putting names to faces. This can be troublesome in both the long and short term, whether it involves forgetting the name of a family member or someone you met at a business meeting. It can be both embarrassing and frustrating, and in extreme cases, such as age-related memory loss, it can become a social handicap, triggered as much because of anxiety over episodes of forgetfulness as from actually suffering from poor memory.

By contrast, if you can learn to overcome these problems and maximize your memory for names and faces, you can boost your self-confidence and self-esteem, and be more assured and relaxed in social situations. If you develop your name–face memory skills to a high level, you can make a real impact by remembering small details about people you've met only briefly. In a social or occupational setting this is an indispensable skill that makes others feel valued and significantly boosts their impression of you.

Distraction and detail

Most forms of memory manage to overcome the obstacle of encoding, so why should names and faces prove so problematic? The stumbling block is distraction: good initial encoding depends on close attention during the early stages of memory formation. Information stored temporarily in short-term memory won't make the transfer unless it's "selected" by the attention process. If your attention is not focused on the information, or the information itself is not inherently attention-grabbing, it will simply be shunted out of the limited-capacity short-term memory and lost.

This is effectively what happens to names in the name–face memory problem. When you are introduced to several people at once—such as at a business meeting—individual names are unlikely to attract sufficient attention to make the transition from short-term to long-term memory.

Linked to this is the fact that a single piece of information, such as a name, is far less likely to make the transition from short-term to long-term memory if it is not backed up by context, associations, and other supporting information. If you are told someone's name in passing or in isolation—e.g., your mother tells you your cousin's wife's name—it will not be backed up by a web of supporting

Name–face associations

Use the visualization and association method to improve your ability to put a name to a face. This involves various ways of thinking of images related to the name.

- Use the person's demeanor or personality to suggest images—e.g., if Jones were hyperactive, you could use an image of a dancing skeleton.

- Think of images that are suggested by the person's face—e.g., "bones" would spring to mind for Jones if Jones's face had prominent cheekbones or heavy brows.

- Find images suggested by the sound of the name—e.g., "Barrett" sounds like "carrot."

Inside the brain:
Synaptic workout

Scientists generally scoff at writers who claim that "your brain is like a muscle—working out can make it bigger and stronger!" But in simple terms this isn't far from the truth. The most basic level of brain organization is the nerve cell, or neuron, which connects with other neurons via synapses (see pages 10–11). When nerve impulses flow around the brain, they travel along neurons and across synapses. The stronger a synaptic connection between two neurons, the more likely it is that a nerve impulse will follow that specific route, and not another route.

Research on simple systems of neurons (taken from sea slugs, which have very big nerve cells) has shown that this relationship also works the other way. The more often a synapse is used, the stronger that synaptic connection becomes—a process called reinforcement.

What does this mean for your memory? Simply that thinking about and using a particular memory will reinforce the synaptic connections involved, helping to embed that memory more strongly in your brain and making it easier to recall. This is how rehearsal and revision work, and why it really is worth repeating something to yourself if you want to remember it.

detail. This can also apply in a multiple-introductions scenario, where there can be too much to take in all at once.

What's in a name?

Another problem with name–face remembering affects a more advanced stage of memory formation—deep encoding to form long-term memories. Successful deep encoding builds webs of association to allow single memories to be accessed from multiple angles. Names pose a challenge to this process, because they are inherently devoid of the most fundamental form of association available—semantic grounding. This is where a word or concept is linked to a concrete reference, such as an object or action, so that it has meaning. Names generally don't possess this quality; the name "Thomas," for instance, does not mean anything in isolation—it has meaning only when associated with a person. This lack of semantic grounding makes names forgettable if they exist in your mind in isolation.

Exercises and strategies to try

Delight your friends

Cultivate the ability to make each person you meet feel valued. Part of this skill stems from being able to remember incidental facts about people, facts that can be brought out and used at will.

- When you first meet someone, make sure that you memorize their name.
- Find out additional details (such as number of children or occupation) through small talk.
- Memorize this information by adding elements to your visualization—e.g., if you meet an attorney, add the image of a judge in full regalia to your visualization of the name.

Make new friends

Don't let poor memory put you off socializing; instead, use new friendships to boost your memory.

- Socializing improves all your mental faculties, helping you to stay sharp.
- Learning about new friends gives you a memory workout as you assimilate details about them.
- Practice learning and remembering information about new friends by using the Maximizer wheel to create a set of "new friends" and information about them so that you can practice gaining and remembering new information.

Pay attention: new names

If you have problems remembering the name of someone you've just been introduced to, follow these tips.

- Pay close attention during an introduction in order to put the name and face of the person you have just met into a physical context, dramatically increasing the amount of detail accessible to you (see Card 5).
- Look carefully at the person whose name you are learning, paying particular attention to their face and physical features.

Recall new names

To better remember a person's name, improve your memory of the first occasion you meet them. Make yourself aware of the following:

- The time and place of the introduction
- The person doing the introduction
- The exact words used
- Any other specific contextual features, such as smell or passers-by, that might make the introduction more memorable

Rehearsal: new names

Rehearse names you've just learned in order to avoid losing them from your short-term memory. Rehearsing names stops them fading from your short-term memory or being displaced by other information. Here are the easiest ways to do it:

- Immediately on hearing the name, repeat the new name back to the person as a sentence—e.g., "Delighted to meet you, Thomas."
- Repeat the name to yourself (not out loud), immediately after and again a short time later.

Identifying the problem and improving memory for names

Difficulties in remembering names and faces stem mainly from problems with the crucial initial encoding stage of the memory process. This is the stage where information stored in short-term memory makes the transition to long-term memory. However, problems may also occur in the subsequent stage of deep encoding to form long-term memory, because names mean so little in isolation. There are three main ways to improve memory for names:

- Changing the way you initially process name–face information, through focusing attention and observation of detail, can enhance initial encoding and promote the transfer of the name from short- to long-term memory.
- Rehearsing name–face information can give this process time to operate before short-term memory-loss processes overwrite it.
- Using visual imagery to make associations helps to improve the quality of both initial and deep encoding, boosting your long-term memory for names and name-related information.

Memory for Everyday Things

 Perhaps the most common and mundane memory problems are those that afflict you in everyday life. Have you ever experienced leaving one room to get something, only to discover on arrival in the next room that you've forgotten what it was you came in for? Or going out to the store and then finding that you've left your wallet at home? Or putting down your keys on getting home, only to realize on your way out that you can't remember where they are? Almost everyone will recognize these common memory problems.

It might not seem worth taking steps to rectify what appear to be minor memory difficulties—but although they may seem trivial, locking yourself out because you forgot to take your keys or finding yourself stranded because you didn't bring any money to pay for a subway ticket can be more than a minor inconvenience. If the misplaced item is something really important, like an inhaler, a "trivial" memory lapse could even be dangerous.

Once you understand the roots of this kind of everyday memory problem, you will be able to overcome the frustration it causes and avoid the petty hassles that may result. There is also a security rationale in ensuring you remember where you left such items as keys, wallet, address book, or cash.

A question of priorities

In fact one of the reasons our minds have evolved to be able to perform automatic tasks such as this is precisely so that we can get on with thinking about more important things, but this has consequences—namely, distraction. Distraction is a common cause of the loss of items from short-term memory. If something distracts you so that you don't rehearse (go over) the action in your mind, your short-term memory of it will rapidly decay, and items such as "remember to pick up the keys" will be lost. A similar process causes the well-known experience of forgetting what you came into the room for. Your original motivation was stored in short-term memory, but a few moments' distraction will prevent rehearsal and leave your mind blank.

The very mundanity of everyday concerns also means that they are easily displaced from short-term memory by more memorable actions, items, or goals. For instance, anxiety about being late is likely to displace from your short-term memory the more mundane and usually automatically monitored issue of whether you have picked up your keys. Everyday items like keys and wallets are easy to lose track of because you tend not to pay attention when you put them down, as it has become an automatic action. You would be less likely to forget where you put your new DVD or your expensive earrings, for instance, because they grab and hold your attention.

The method of loci

Your familiarity with the everyday aspects of your environment could prove to be of enormous benefit to your memory skills, because it forms the basis for a classic mnemonic strategy known as the method of loci (loci means "places" in Greek). This strategy was widely used by the ancient Greeks, in particular for remembering long speeches or stories, but is also ideally suited for tasks like memorizing shopping lists.

The method of loci involves using a mental map of an environment you are familiar enough with that you can easily recall its layout and the placement of items within it. It could be your home, your yard, a route you often take (e.g., your route to work), a park you know well, or even just a familiar room. During the Renaissance, scholars suggested such diverse mnemonic loci as the layout of an Elizabethan theater or the stops along the route of the pilgrimage to Jerusalem.

Once you have settled on the environment you will use, picture a range of different locations within it (e.g., the rooms of a house) and mentally travel through them in a specific order. This order is important, which is why picking a familiar route or journey is a good idea. Your chosen environment can now serve as a framework on which to "hang" associations and visualizations of things that you want to remember.

This method can also be used to remember anything that can be divided up into stages or chunks, such as a speech or an essay. You simply need to come up with a key word, phrase, or image for each part of it. Use the method of loci to recall each key in turn, and use the keys to trigger the appropriate part of the speech or essay. Because you can easily recall the order of locations in the house or your chosen environment, you will also be able to remember the parts of your speech or essay in the right order.

Exercises and strategies to try

Review five times

Repeating information is a tried-and-tested means to memory success. This technique can be used to help memorize relatively complex material such as a speech or facts for an essay.

- Repeat information five times to fix it in your memory, making the repetitions at progressively longer intervals—after an hour, then after a day, then after a week, then after two weeks, and finally after a month.

Number–rhyme system

Take a leaf out of children's books and employ a number–rhyme system to memorize short strings of numbers using simple rhymes suggested by the numbers. Make up your own rhymes or use the rhymes below then turn the words into a story or visualize them as objects along a route, putting the rhyming words in the appropriate order.

Create a narrative scenario using the following rhyming peg words in the correct order for the number sequence you are memorizing:

1 = sun	6 = tricks
2 = pew	7 = heaven
3 = me	8 = plate
4 = roar	9 = pine
5 = dive	0 = hero

Number–word system

A good way to memorize security numbers is to convert them into a sentence in which the length of each word in the sentence is determined by the relevant digit. For example, if your PIN number were 3734 you'd make up a phrase or sentence with words that were three letters, then seven letters, then three letters, and finally four letters long. Try to use memorable words, such as

"big, hideous, and ugly"   or

"bad manners are rude."

Peg word system: short

Use a rhyming peg word system to remember lists in a particular order. Each peg word rhymes with a number that indicates the position of the item in the list, so the rhyming word becomes a "peg" for an association. The first list gives peg words for a list of up to ten items, but you could make up your own instead.

1 = bun	6 = sticks
2 = shoe	7 = heaven
3 = tree	8 = gate
4 = door	9 = wine
5 = hive	10 = hen

So to remember the order in which a set of ten cards was dealt, you might picture the queen of hearts (which had been dealt first) eating a bun, the five of spades (dealt second) wearing a shoe, etc.

For lists of up to 20 items, you will need to learn another ten peg words in addition to those above. These peg words here have been selected because their sounds are close to the sounds of the numbers they are pegged to.

11 = leaven	16 = pristine
12 = shelf	17 = setting
13 = hurting	18 = waiting
14 = boarding	19 = knighting
15 = fitting	20 = plenty

As an example, if you need to remember that Spain was the eleventh country in a list of countries, you could imagine a toreador making bread by adding leaven.

To create peg words for numbers from 21 to 100, combine the pegs for multiples of 10 with those for numbers 1–9. The words chosen here are mostly adjectives, to make them easier to combine with nouns—for example, 32 would be "flirty shoe." Remember, you can always make up your own alternatives.

20 plenty	70 pleasantly
30 flirty	80 weighty
40 naughty	90 mighty
50 nifty	100 sundered
60 sexy	

Alternative peg systems

Instead of peg words relating to numbers this peg word system uses the order of the 26 letters of the alphabet. It can therefore be used for remembering lists of up to 26 items. Memorize the peg words overleaf (or come up with your own), which can then be pegged to each item on lists you need to remember.

A = ape	J = jail	S = sun
B = beach	K = kite	T = teepee
C = cat	L = log	U = unicorn
D = dog	M = mail	V = villa
E = egg	N = net	W = wig
F = feather	O = owl	X = Xmas
G = genie	P = pig	Y = yacht
H = hedge	Q = quilt	Z = zoo
I = ice	R = rain	

A rhyming peg system works in the same way, with a list consisting of words that rhyme, or part-rhyme, with the letters of the alphabet, which you may find easier to remember. Again, you can come up with your own list of peg "rhymes" if they suit you better.

A = hay	J = jade	S = eskimo
B = bee	K = key	T = tea
C = sea	L = elbow	U = ewe
D = deed	M = hem	V = veal
E = eagle	N = hen	W = double you
F = effort	O = oboe	X = X-ray
G = jeep	P = pea	Y = wire
H = age	Q = queue	Z = zebra
I = eye	R = oar	

The calendar peg system is the same but the words are associated (through sound or meaning) with the 12 months of the year. This system can therefore be used for remembering the order of up to 12 events in a year, such as "Daddy dune and Mommy Santa" for your parents' birthdays.

January = jacket

February = freeze

March = march

April = bunny

May = flowers

June = dune

July = jungle

August = barbecue

September = scepter

October = Doberman

November = bonfire

December = Santa Claus

Overlearn for success

For something you really need to remember, repeat it beyond the point at which you think you know it. Memorizing something to this degree is known as overlearning—repetitive learning of material beyond what is needed for initial learning. It is particularly useful for training in music or other physical skills because it helps complex actions become automatic, which makes remembering them much easier.

Storytelling strategy

When wading through reams of class notes or boring textbooks, stop your attention from tending to wander by making the material into a story.

- Relate the characters or incidents to key words, so that the order of the narrative matches the order of the facts you need to remember, such as steps in a cycle of chemical reactions.
- Brainstorm your own ideas for the most exciting stories you can create that relate to the material that you are trying to learn.

Be a human say-planner

Try this mnemonic technique to remember friends' and relatives' significant dates.

- Combine calendar peg words with the peg words for numbers 1–31 to visualize any day of the year.
- Add the person to the mix, with something appropriate (such as their "birthday suit").
- For example, you could visualize your friend Neil's birthday on Feb. 11 ("freeze" + "leaven") as a naked Neil trying to take a loaf out of the ice-filled larder.
- Once you've committed to memory all the relevant associations, you can summon up your visualization for all your personally important days of the year to find out what happens on that day.

Team tactics for recall

Are you a sports buff who has an encyclopedic memory for sporting trivia but keeps forgetting domestic and personal information? If so turn this knowledge of trivia to your advantage by using it as a mnemonic aid.

If you know your team by heart, use it to provide pegs for visualizations, especially when you have to remember things in a particular order. Write down the players and their numbers and then visualize each one with the elements of what you need to remember, such as the names of new colleagues. Base your mental pictures on either names or looks.

Use the power of laughter

Amusing associations and visualizations are the most memorable, so where possible, make up something that will make you laugh. The more ridiculous it is, the better.

- For example, to remember items you want to buy at the grocery store, imagine a face made up of the different fruits you need.

- If you are using the memory-house or memory-journey method to remember the weekly shopping list, and you need detergent for the dishes, imagine the family caught up in giant soap bubbles bouncing around the kitchen.

Aide-mémoires

Adopt a classic aide-mémoire—a physical memory-booster that puts retrieval cues into concrete form—to help remember what you need when you are on the move:

- Lists
- Knots tied in a handkerchief
- Rosary beads
- An alarm clock
- Post-It Notes

And why not make up your own? Use an object you will see every day to act as a trigger.

Give your keys a home

Avoid the problem of losing everyday things like keys by adopting a new routine.

- Pick a "home" spot where they can "live," and make a habit of always putting them down there when you come in. If you forget, do it as soon as you realize, and it will soon become a habit.

- Or try this technique: whenever you go out, get into the habit of pocket-patting, key-jangling, or some other process involving the items you need to take with you. You may soon stop noticing that you're doing it—until the keys are absent or the pockets are empty, when the disruption to your new routine should prompt you to pick up the offending item.

Through the keyhole

Another good way to remember important things you need to take as you leave home. Think of a visualization that incorporates the door, the keyhole, the handle, or some other aspect that you can't avoid as you go out.

Turning the handle, turning the key in the lock, or opening the door will then trigger the visualization so that you will recall what it was that you needed to remember.

This method can also help when you're out and you think of things you need to remember when you return, since you have to go through the same process on re-entering your home. A key-based mental picture will prove especially handy.

Use concrete solutions

Also try one of these physical solutions to help you remember items you need to take with you when leaving the house:

- Leave the items in a location clearly visible by the front door, so that they catch your eye when you are leaving.

- Stick a note to the front door reminding you to check that you've got everything you need.

- Arrange things so that you have to interact physically with the items or the spot where you left them—e.g., place the hall table in front of the door, so you have to stop and move it! That way, your unthinking routine when you leave the house will become less automatic.

Episodic Memory

Your memory for events, conversations, actions, situations, or other "episodes" that have happened in the past, known as episodic memory, plays a vital role in everyday life as well as contributing in a profound way to your personal psychology. Forgetting things that have happened can be irritating and occasionally embarrassing. It hampers, for instance, your ability to recall facts, tell stories, describe places, and remember names and faces.

A particular type of episodic memory, autobiographical memory, is your memory for the events that make up your life. This is important to your psychology at a profound level, because it is essential to your sense of identity—your sense of who you are and your place in the world.

If your autobiographical memory is poor, you are more likely to feel, perhaps at a subconscious level, that you are somehow missing out on part of life, or may feel

Identifying the problem and fixing episodic memory

There are several possible causes for poor episodic memory. One factor is probably genetic: some people simply have a better memory than others, just as some are more intelligent. Memory ability in this sense is probably something to do with the ability of neurons in the brain to form and maintain connections. A more serious culprit, which you can easily take steps to counteract, is poor encoding—problems with the stage at which short-term memories are laid down as longer-term ones. Another major factor is lifestyle, as lack of sleep, stress, alcohol, and drugs can all affect episodic memory.

There are two primary avenues you can follow to improve your episodic memory. The first is to work prospectively—planning ahead—to improve your encoding of episodic memories, so that when you come to recall them in the future, your abilities are enhanced. The second is to use various strategies to boost your recall retrospectively—i.e., for episodic memory that you've already laid down.

Memory mystery:

Why do the elderly remember episodes from their youth, but forget what they did yesterday?

One of the most remarkable features of memory is that it often seems to defy logic, so that people who struggle to remember day-to-day events can picture with absolute clarity things that happened to them decades ago. One reason for this is that most of the long-term memories that can be vividly recalled carry particular emotional resonance, and episodes such as this are, by their very nature, likely to be deeply encoded and therefore longer-lasting.

In addition, old memories were laid down when the brain's faculties were at full strength, and over the years they have crystallized into permanently stored memory traces deeply embedded in the gray matter of the brain. New memories, by contrast, don't enjoy high-quality initial encoding because the brain's faculties are no longer at full strength, and so they never get the chance to become fully embedded memory traces in the brain.

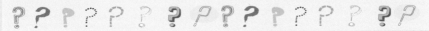

confused about your identity. When your autobiographical recall is working well, you have a strong sense of identity and thus feel more confident. This is one reason we are often jealous of those with perfect autobiographical recall.

Causes of poor encoding

- One reason for poor encoding is simply lack of rehearsal. Failure to review (think over or replay in your mind) events after they've occurred makes them less likely to be laid down in long-term memory storage.

- Another cause of poor encoding is failure to give events your full "sensory attention" at the time. This doesn't mean that you're not aware of what's going on, but rather that you may not be fully engaged with all your senses. For instance, if you're at a party, you might be focused mainly on the music, on the snacks that are on offer, or on chatting to a friend, and not on the guest list or the layout of the host's home.

- Yet another common reason for poor encoding of episodes is that they may not be particularly memorable. If you are stuck in a rut or are caught in a routine, particularly one that is not mentally or physically taxing, such as sitting in front of the television every night, or doing a dull, repetitive job, the episodes of your life may quite naturally run together in your mind.

Lifestyle factors

Finally, look to your lifestyle. Lack of sleep affects memory formation adversely, and many psychologists believe that sleep is essential for "mental housekeeping" processes, such as reinforcing memories laid down during the day.

High levels of stress, apart from exacerbating sleep problems, won't help, partly because you might end up focusing heavily on one aspect of your life to the detriment of memory formation for other areas.

A more-than-moderate use of alcohol, and virtually any level of use of recreational drugs, also impairs memory performance by disrupting encoding processes. For more about the effects of lifestyle on memory, see pages 102–125.

How to boost encoding

One way to achieve better encoding of episodic memories is through "mindfulness"—the ability to pay attention to an experience, without losing focus because of interrupting thoughts and concerns about the past, the future, or other locations or activities. Mindfulness can produce a richer sensory picture of an event, giving your memory more to work with and thus strengthening the encoding process.

Challenging your recall abilities

If you describe yourself as having a terrible memory, you may be tempted to dismiss your powers of episodic memory recall without challenging them. However, with a bit of effort you could surprise yourself. Once you get started on remembering, it can be impressive how much comes back to you.

Improving the quality of the episodes that make up your life will literally make them more memorable. Engage in engrossing and challenging pursuits, and break out of stale routines. This is particularly important for older people—keeping active mentally, physically, and socially helps preserve memory and other mental faculties.

Memory for facts and figures

Knowledge is a form of memory. Facts and figures, dates and places—these are types of semantic memory. Not all problems with knowledge are linked to memory; lack of knowledge may be caused by educational factors instead. But a common and frus-

trating difficulty with knowledge is the scenario in which you know that you do know something, but you can't quite remember it! This is a sensation experienced by anyone who has answered trivia quiz questions, struggled with a crossword puzzle, or taken an exam, with consequences ranging from mere irritation to serious academic upset.

Identifying and fixing problems with memory for facts and figures

Recall of facts and figures is problematic because of the difficulties in achieving high-quality, rich encoding of the information in the first place. This difficulty with quality encoding particularly applies to numbers, which, as abstract symbols, suffer from a similar problem to names—an absence of semantic grounding, linking them to concrete references. In other words, numbers aren't memorable.

Adopt these strategies to make facts and figures memorable.

- For facts, use such tricks as visualization-association, material review, and changing the presentation. These involve improving the way you encode this material so you are fitting them into a wider framework of knowledge.

- For specific types of knowledge, such as spelling, adapt mnemonic strategies.

- For numbers, the key is to transform them into more memorable forms, using systems based on shape, letters, rhymes, and "associations."

Memory for numbers, dates, and statistics overlaps with this memory for other facts. However, it also encompasses other types of semantic memory. Common problems in this sphere include difficulties remembering phone numbers, people's birthdays, alarm-deactivating sequences, and lock combinations.

Creating a framework

Quality encoding of data to long-term memory means not simply learning facts in isolation but understanding them and how they relate to larger factual structures and systems, so that accessing the data from multiple avenues becomes possible.

For example, you might find it hard to recall, in isolation, that the U.S. President in 1918 was Woodrow Wilson. However, it would be easier to remember if you also knew that 1918 was the year World War I ended and that one of his primary legacies was helping to draw up the peace treaty that ended the war. Understanding information in this way boosts your recall of both the information and its associated framework.

Do your exercises

Crossword puzzles, word games, and trivia quizzes provide excellent mental workouts that will improve your recall for facts and figures and your overall mental agility. If you have difficulty with dates or historical facts, start by using photos, old day-planners, and newspapers as memory props and prompters.

Exercises and strategies to try

Instant review

Use this valuable memory-boosting trick to help prevent important information from being lost from short-term memory before it has time to transfer to long-term memory. It is particularly useful when talking to other people.

- Train yourself to review, or mentally repeat, data soon after you've encountered it. This will dramatically improve your recall of phone numbers, social arrangements, and directions, as well as people's names.

- If being introduced to someone, ask the person their name again if you need to. At this early stage, it is a reasonable request that won't cause embarrassment.

Memory master card trick

Use this memory masters' party trick to impress your friends or gain an advantage at card games.

- Remember cards as they are dealt by combining attributes of each card with a memorable association, in this case using a celebrity (or, if you prefer, a made-up character). As examples of the associations you can make, the ten of diamonds could be a flash hip-hop star with big diamond rings on every finger and thumb.

- To help further, visualize each in a vivid setting such as a lifeboat, then imagine them interacting.

Memory visualizations

Improve your own geographical and navigational memory with this exercise, using the streets in your neighborhood. Test yourself as often as possible, both physically and in your imagination.

1 As you walk or drive, visualize your route as it would look on a map.

2 Use primary landmarks as markers to help you recall routes between less well-known locations.

3 From a map of your area, select obscure locations, and take imaginary journeys between them by visualizing what the trips would look like, paying particular attention to main streets and landmarks with which you are familiar.

Remember directions quickly

Asking someone for directions poses a memory challenge, because you have to remember a series of "left" and "right" instructions while navigating through an unfamiliar place. To make the task easier, use each left and right as the basis for words or names, which you can then form into a sentence.

- For a left followed by a right, use LarRy or LauRa.
- For a right followed by a left, use RoLls or RuLer.
- For a left followed by a left, use LoLa.
- For a right followed by a right, use RoaRs or RoaRing.
- Use the words in a sentence. For example, "right, right, left, right, right, left, left, right" becomes "RoaRing LarRy RoLls over LauRa."

Find your way fast

To remember a complicated series of directions like "third on the left, then second on the right, then right again," substitute a set of more memorable concepts or a system you know which falls into a system or can be woven into a narrative. If you are a chess buff, for instance, you could use the different pieces, with their different moves, to represent directions, as explained overleaf.

- Visualize white pieces for left-hand turns and black ones for right-hand turns.
- "Go straight along" could be a rook, because rooks move in straight lines.
- "First left" could be a pawn, because pawns can move diagonally ahead.
- "Second left, first right" could be a knight.

Phone bill review

Episodic memory—your memory for things that you've done—isn't just about your distant past.

It's important to remember the more recent past as well. Give your memory a workout using an itemized phone bill. Sit down with your next bill and work backward through the list of numbers. With each number, see if you can remember whom you rang, what the call was about, and anything else you talked about.

Brain-boosting Strategies

You can also boost your memory to maximize your performance on IQ tests. Start by honing basic mental skills then make brain-boosting strategies part of your everyday life by applying them in work and domestic settings to help boost your performances in these fields.

Improve your mental speed

The most general ability of all is g, the hypothetical "general intelligence" factor that probably underlies all types of intelligence and is so important to your performance on IQ tests. While g is closely linked to overall measures of intelligence, such as that provided by a standard, complete IQ test, there is a lot of evidence to suggest that it relates differently to the various subtypes of intelligence we all possess. In other words, there are some subtypes that seem to involve more g than others.

The evidence suggests that there is a strong relationship between g and numerical–mathematical intelligence (NMI), which is the subtype that involves being able to manipulate numbers and understand the relationships between numbers and similar abstract concepts. This means that your performance in an NMI exercise is probably a fairly good measure of the strength or power of your g factor—in other words, it provides a cunning way to get an almost direct look at g. NMI exercises can take several different forms, which vary in complexity—and difficulty.

A simple measure of intellectual power

Let's start with a simple, straightforward NMI exercise, called Countdown. A test of numerical ability, the exercise involves little or no reasoning or other forms of advanced thinking, but its very simplicity may help to make it a good measure of g. Your performance in this exercise basically depends on brute mental strength, which, of course, is pretty much what g is.

Improve your crystallized intelligence

Although IQ tests are supposedly designed to test only ability and not achievement, aptitude and not knowledge, certain types of question do involve what might be called crystallized intelligence. Some IQ tests even include general-knowledge

Countdown

Countdown is an exercise in mental arithmetic, in the guise of mental subtraction. Simply pick a number between 93 and 99 and subtract 7 from it repeatedly, in your head, until you get to 0 or less. That's all there is to it. Time yourself and record how long it takes you to reach 0. Do this five times when you first read this book, and work out the average time. Make a note of it.

As you work through this book and the exercises, come back to this simple exercise and repeat it to see if there's any sign of progress. On each occasion, do the exercise five times, timing yourself on each trial, and then take the average of the five trials. If your time comes down (i.e., you get faster), it strongly suggests that your g factor is sharpening and your mental speed is increasing, thanks to the IQ-workout program.

questions. So learning and reading may well improve your performance on some types of questions. This could be through boosting your vocabulary and your knowledge of how words relate to one another (important for verbal-aptitude questions such as those involving synonyms and antonyms) or through teaching you precepts of logic or typical pitfalls of false reasoning.

Some numerical–mathematical skills need to be learned as well—for example, some questions require you to use simultaneous equations, which few people are able to master without at least rudimentary training.

Improve your working memory

Short-term memory, also known as working memory, is involved in many problem-solving tasks, especially when you take in information and need to keep it in mind for a short period, perhaps while performing other mental operations on it.

For example, in order to perform mental arithmetic you need to take in the numbers in the calculation being presented to you, and then store them briefly somewhere in your mind so that they are available for multiplication, addition, subtraction, or division—that "somewhere" is working memory. Similarly, when you scan a series of shapes so that you can predict the next in the series, you store the existing shapes in your working memory while your analytical functions operate on them. Improving your working-memory ability could help to boost your performance on a range of IQ-style questions, from mental arithmetic to logical analysis.

Memory exercises

The most basic working-memory exercise, which is used in its own right as part of some IQ tests, is the digit-span test. On average, working memory can store up to seven bits of information, such as numbers, names, letters, or phonemes (parts of spoken language). Practice the test and you may be able to boost your digit-span by one or two numbers. Alternatively, working on basic memory-boosting strategies such as visualization and association will enhance your basic memory abilities.

Improve your creativity

Creative thinking and its close relation, lateral thinking (solving problems by an indirect or unusual approach), are often associated with highly intelligent people. They can be particularly helpful when it comes to answering tough questions or spotting well-concealed patterns or solutions, because they help to free the mind from strictures and unproductive patterns of thought.

Free your mind

For instance, look at this anagram: REACTIVE. Can you solve it? How long did it take? This is not a particularly difficult anagram—its solution requires the rearrangement of just one letter—but it is perfectly natural to struggle with it because of the way the human mind works. Our minds have evolved to see and latch on to patterns, an ability that makes us good at creating order out of chaos and deriving meaning from limited information. (This is something that even the most cutting-edge artificial intelligence and computer systems struggle with.) But the downside is that once you've latched on to a pattern it can be very hard to put it out of your mind. In this instance that pattern is the existing word "reactive," which intrudes and prevents you from visualizing the actual solution. The anagram might be easier to solve if it were presented in a form that didn't make sense as a word in its own right, which is precisely why most anagrams are not presented like this.

Divergent and convergent thinking

This is where creative thinking comes in. The creative mind is better able to step

outside—or aside from (hence "lateral" thinking)—"stuck" patterns. Psychologists call this divergent thinking, as opposed to convergent thinking. In the anagram example, a creative approach is mentally to jumble up the letters and come at them from new angles, to visualize them in new ways. This will free your mind from the strictures naturally imposed upon it by the form of the question.

Boost Your CQ

Some psychologists have sought to recognize the importance of creativity by testing and measuring it to provide a "creative quotient," or CQ, comparable to IQ. Although the study is still in its infancy, training your creative-thinking skills will potentially get you into a more creative frame of mind prior to attempting IQ-style questions.

Categories

The first exercise is a very simple one involving making lists. All you have to do is choose a category (such as types of fruit or girls' names—it could be anything) and see how many examples of it you can come up with in a set time. It may be easier if you have a friend to time you and count the number of examples you call out (while disregarding repetitions). It doesn't really matter how many you get, although you might like to compete with your friend. Bear in mind that some categories are easier than others—for example, "animals" is easier than "fruit."

The aim is simply to practice broadening the scope of your recall beyond the usual, prototypical examples. For example, if the category is "animals," most people will say "lion," "dog," or "elephant," but few will say "toucan," "iguana," or "tsetse fly." Perhaps you can devise a scoring system that rewards what psychologists call "flexibility" (the range and exoticism of your examples) as well as "fluency" (the number of examples).

The "uses" game

A related game is used by psychologists at the University of Sydney as a test of what they call "ideational fluency," and from which they derive CQ measurements. It involves getting someone to come up with as many uses as possible for an item. The actual item is not particularly important; what matters is the fluency and flexibility of your responses—how many uses you come up with and how creative they are. For example, try to think of as many uses as possible for a box of matches, and be as creative as possible. Write them down, and then consider the nature of your answers—did you concentrate mainly on things you could do with the matches, or

Navigating the problem space

Imagine the process of arriving at the solution to a problem as being like groping your way through a maze and trying to find the most promising avenues, which might eventually lead to the correct answer. This kind of creative or lateral thinking lets you step beyond or around the most obvious or accessible solution pathways, which are actually dead ends, and find shortcuts to the correct paths.

with the matches in conjunction with the box? Divergent thinkers are more likely to have included answers that involved emptying out the matches and using just the box, but many people do not make the creative leap. This is a literal example of thinking out of the box, a form of creative thinking much favored by management consultants, but it can also help you to solve difficult puzzles.

Improve your critical thinking

Logical thinking is one of the main abilities tested in an IQ test and impacts on other mental abilities as well. One of the key elements of logical thinking is what is known as critical thinking. Fundamentally, critical thinking is about challenging assumptions and using reason, not false reasoning, to guide you.

Assumptions

Many of our thought processes start from the basis of assumptions, which may be unhelpful or misleading. For example, a lot of people when faced with a math problem automatically throw up their hands and assume they can't possibly manage it. This becomes a self-fulfilling prophecy, in the sense that they never learn to cope with math problems—psychologists call it learned helplessness. Challenging the assumption that they can't do it is the first step toward overcoming the difficulty.

On a different level, assumptions can hinder you when navigating the problem space toward a solution, by setting you off on the wrong path to begin with. For example, when confronted by a series of groups of letters and asked to predict the next one in the series, you might begin with an assumption that the groups must be a code for real words, or that the relation between them must be to do with the alphabet. In fact, the answer might be something totally different (such as all the letters being worth one point in the board game Scrabble). Your assumptions have hamstrung you from the start.

Critical thinking really comes into its own when you are trying to solve logic problems, where the most obvious answer may not be correct. For example, it is common to assume that the question does not provide all the information you need to answer it, when a closer look might reveal that it does.

The other main aspect of critical thinking is being alert to and thus avoiding errors in reasoning, known as fallacies. A typical fallacy is the "argument from authority," where it is assumed that a claim must be true because it is being made by an "authority," when, in fact, the one doesn't necessarily have anything to do with the other.

As regards IQ-style questions, fallacies can mislead you when you are answering straight logic questions (such as questions of the "true or false" variety), and they can make it hard to solve problems involving logical progressions. A good example is the fallacy of division, which is where you assume that what is true of part must be true of the whole. If you look at a series of shapes with dots in each corner and are asked to predict the next in the series, you might assume that just because the difference between the first two shapes is that the dot moves clockwise, this must be true of the whole series. You might then fail to test this assumption properly by checking the other shapes in the series.

It's beyond the scope of this book to give a full list of fallacies, but the point is that training in answering IQ-style questions can improve your critical-thinking skills; and better critical thinking, particularly getting into the habit of questioning assumptions, can improve your performance on IQ-style tests.

Identifying and fixing bad memory

One reason that everyday actions are hard to remember is that they become routine. When you repeat the same set of actions in much the same order you will inevitably no longer focus your full attention on your actions or on what you need to recall.

Solutions to everyday memory loss need not be too troublesome   A sensible approach is that if you know you can't trust your memory, then don't! Work around your memory problems, making allowances for them. Do this by adopting new routines, finding aide-mémoires, and using your environment to interrupt automatic processes, as well as more conventional memory-boosting strategies such as focusing attention and making quick and easy associations.

Go to page 164 to find a series of tests and exercises that will improve the various different types of memory.

Part Three

The Brain Power Lifestyle

Memory and Lifestyle

Ensuring optimal performance for your memory isn't just about boosting it with mnemonic strategies and working it out with memorization exercises. You also need to preserve the memory abilities that you possess by keeping your brain in good working order and protecting it against the insults life throws at it. In this section we'll see how your lifestyle, including diet, sleep, and exercise, can affect your mental powers both positively and negatively.

Maintaining your cardiovascular health isn't simply good for your heart. It can also help to ensure a steady supply of blood to your brain, which helps to keep your nerve cells thriving and to protect your mental abilities.

Protecting your memory

Some of the connections between lifestyle and memory are obvious—most people are acquainted with the amnesiac effects of a night of heavy drinking, for instance. Other factors are more subtle, such as the scheduling of your sleep routine or the part that music plays in your life.

Alcohol and drugs

Anything bad for your physical health will also be detrimental to your intellectual health, so drinking heavily or using drugs is likely to affect your memory abilities adversely. Alcohol can damage the brain directly by killing off nerve cells, although there is evidence that, in moderation, alcohol can have some positive health effects. Red wine, for instance, is known to contain chemicals that act as antioxidants. Alcohol causes intoxication by interfering with the flow of electrical impulses around the brain. That's why getting drunk makes you feel befuddled. One effect of this is to disrupt the formation of memories, so that it's often difficult to remember what happened to you while you were drunk. In recent experiments, test subjects who learned material after drinking alcohol suffered from poor recall when tested later.

However, the same scientists also found that material learned before the subjects got drunk was actually recalled better than normal on testing the next day. One explanation for this effect might be that the lack of memory formation in the interval between learning and testing, as a result of the memory-damping effects of alcohol, meant that there was no interference effect (see page 61). Although interesting, this finding should probably not be taken as a handy revision tip, since the test material involved was quite simple. Memory for the complex material you need to learn for exams or presentations would almost certainly suffer from a night of drinking, not to mention the effects of a hangover on mental performance.

Recreational drugs are thought to be detrimental to memory. Although cocaine might cause temporary memory improvement, there is a hangover effect afterward. Cannabis in particular adversely affects memory, and can cause quite severe memory problems for regular users. Drug use is also bad for your general health, increasing the levels of free radicals in your system and thus prematurely aging your brain.

Smoking

Nicotine, the main addictive ingredient in tobacco, has some short-lived effects on mental processes that mean some smokers find that a cigarette temporarily sharpens their thinking and memory. However, the many negatives heavily outweigh any transient benefits.

Smoking is a major threat to your cardiovascular health and therefore to your memory. Cigarette smoke contains a lot of carbon monoxide, which is absorbed easily in the lungs and competes with oxygen for binding spots on the hemoglobin molecules in your red blood cells. In fact carbon monoxide binds to hemoglobin much more strongly than oxygen, so inhaling cigarette smoke can significantly reduce the amount of oxygen getting to your brain. Smoking also boosts production of free radicals—reactive molecules that can damage DNA and cell machinery, thereby directly damaging brain tissue.

Heart of the matter

Lifestyle issues have a specific impact on the brain and on memory, but they also have a more general impact via their effect on cardiovascular health. Your brain is probably the greediest organ in your body, in terms of its demands for fuel and oxygen. Although it accounts for just 2 percent of body mass, it receives 14 percent of the body's blood flow, soaks up no less than 20 percent of the oxygen taken in by the lungs, and uses a full 60 percent of the body's glucose supply. To feed its voracious appetite, the brain requires a rich and constant blood supply, and anything that threatens to disrupt this supply is a threat to brain function, including memory.

Goal checklist ✔
Why I'm going to quit smoking

Read these health dangers whenever you feel like a cigarette:

- ☐ Accelerated deposits of cholesterol in arteries, causing high blood pressure, cardiovascular disease, stroke, angina, impotence
- ☐ Increased risk of cancer of lung, mouth, and throat
- ☐ Damage to senses of taste and smell; foul breath
- ☐ Reduced oxygen supply to brain, causing poor memory and concentration, and accelerated cognitive decline
- ☐ Improved performance for memory, attention, and learning, and delayed cognitive decline
- ☐ Increased fitness levels, endurance, speed, and strength
- ☐ Increased life span
- ☐ Increased sexual potency
- ☐ Enhanced senses of taste and smell
- ☐ Reduced risk of cancer

Memory under stress

Stress affects general health by disrupting sleep and exacerbating cardiovascular problems (high stress levels have been linked to conditions such as arteriosclerosis and high blood pressure), which, in turn, is bad news for memory performance. And although a little stress can boost memory, most people find that too much stress makes it hard to concentrate, which in turn adversely affects the encoding stage of memory. Anxiety also makes recall more difficult, and it can increase the chances of "blocking."

By contrast, relaxation helps overcome these problems. Achieving a relaxed state of mind allows recall to flow more easily. The next time you find yourself struggling to remember a particular experience, make a conscious effort to overcome the block with a relaxation exercise. The exercises on pages 177–78 describe specific memory-boosting meditations. If you practice enough, you will lower your anxiety levels, enhance your ability to relax while under stress, and boost your memory powers.

Lifestyle and the brain

Diet is just one aspect of your lifestyle, which incorporates everything about how you live, what you do to your body, and what you put into it. Factors that adversely affect your mental abilities are those that impair your brain's health by reducing the supply of blood, oxygen, and nutrients, exposing it to toxins, and not giving it sufficient time and materials for self-maintenance and repair. Lifestyle factors that enhance your mental functioning are those that boost blood supply to the brain, reduce its exposure to toxins, and give it the time and materials to look after itself.

Lack of sleep, and caffeine, can have as detrimental effects as nicotine, alcohol, and drugs. Conversely, exercise boosts brain health by improving circulation and lung capacity, and therefore the supply of oxygen and nutrients to the brain. It improves mood, and has been shown to be as effective against depression as antidepressants while relaxation skills can also improve mental health.

Mini-strokes

A major interruption of blood supply to the brain as a result of a blocked or burst vessel is known as a stroke. Far more frequent, however, are mini-strokes, caused by transient interruptions of the blood supply or failures of tiny capillaries (the smallest blood vessels, with a diameter equal to the width of one blood cell). These are linked to cardiovascular problems such as arteriosclerosis (the buildup of deposits on the inside of arteries, restricting blood flow, raising blood pressure, and causing blockages when chunks break off and are carried into smaller blood vessels), high blood pressure, and poor oxygenation of the blood (as a result of reduced lung function).

When problems such as these interrupt or restrict blood flow to the brain, they cause nerve cells to die off. Perhaps only a tiny number die off at a time, so that there is no way you could notice it, but the damage is cumulative. This may be responsible for a lot of age-related decline in mental functions, particularly in memory abilities. Losing nerve cells causes the degradation of the networks of cells that represent stored memories, making them harder to access and leading in turn to the degradation and eventual loss of those memories.

Sleeping and Relaxation

 Sleeping is universal across almost the entire animal kingdom. Worms do not sleep, but even fish have "rest" periods of lowered physiological and neural activity. Humans spend around a third of their lives sleeping. Sleep deprivation is distressing and rapidly fatal—after 60 hours you would experience significant mental deficits, after around four days hallucinations, and eventually death.

The function of sleep

Evidently sleep is important, yet we still do not know exactly what it is for. Several different functions have been suggested, which may all be true to varying extents. The main purposes of sleep are thought to be:

- Bodily restoration: Sleep restores bodily energy levels and allows restorative processes time to work.
- Mental restoration: Sleep is necessary for maintenance of mental energy levels.
- Learning and memory: Sleep is when information absorbed during the day is consolidated, and some of the total information is jettisoned in a kind of mental housekeeping.

The structure of sleep

By observing sleepers in laboratory conditions and recording their brain activity, eye movements, muscle tension, and breathing, psychologists have discovered that there are different kinds of sleep and that a typical night's sleep follows a characteristic pattern.

Ordinary sleep

When you first drop off to sleep, you enter Stage 1 of what is called non-rapid eye movement (NREM) sleep. This stage is light sleep, from which you are easily woken. After around seven minutes you drop into Stage 2 sleep, and over the next 10–25 minutes you fall into Stage 3, and then Stage 4, or deep sleep. During Stage 4 sleep, most brain activity slows right down, and only the brain stem—the part of the brain that controls basic functions, such as breathing—continues to operate normally.

REM sleep

After a period of deep sleep, your brain stem sends out arousal signals and prods your cerebral cortex back into consciousness, albeit a special form of consciousness. You are now entering the fifth phase of sleep—rapid eye movement (REM) sleep, when dreams take place.

During REM sleep, your conscious mind is cut off from your senses and your muscles (except for the eye muscles), so that you cannot act out your dreams. Sometimes this protective mechanism fails, and the result is sleeptalking, or even sleepwalking. Even in normal sleep some level of your consciousness remains wired up to the outside world—for example, if a telephone rings, the sound may be incorporated into your dream.

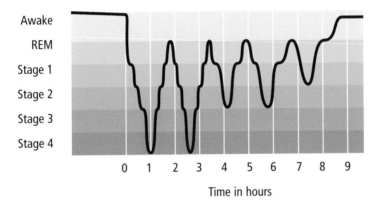

Time in hours

The sleep cycle

An adult generally passes through the five phases of sleep roughly every 90 minutes (above), although the time spent in each phase changes over the course of the night, and over the course of a life. When you first drop off, you spend more time in deep sleep and only a couple of minutes in REM sleep, but by the next morning your REM phases may be up to 30 minutes long.

Healthy sleep habits

Men need, on average, eight hours' sleep a night to feel properly rested, while women need seven. If you get less than this, you start to suffer side effects during waking hours—impaired concentration and memory, learning difficulties, mental slowness, impaired reactions, co-ordination, and movement, and, of course, fatigue.

Contrary to popular belief, however, you cannot simply make up sleep deficits by sleeping for longer at weekends. In fact, sleeping late can disrupt your normal sleeping patterns, making things worse. Here are a few healthy sleeping habits you should practice:

- Try to get your recommended daily amount of sleep.
- Go to bed when you feel tired.
- Prepare for sleep by avoiding eating or overstimulating activities, like watching TV, just beforehand.
- Keep TVs, computers, work, and so on out of your bedroom. Bedrooms should be used only for sleeping and sex.
- Stick to a regular sleep routine, including at weekends.
- Avoid alcohol, cigarettes, and caffeine for at least four hours before bedtime—they interfere with healthy sleeping patterns so that you don't get the full benefit.
- People with chronic snoring should consult a physician or sleep specialist to make sure they are not suffering from sleep apnea, a condition that interferes with healthy sleeping patterns and can cause fatigue.
- Practice relaxation techniques to help prevent stress-related insomnia.

Dreams

You can have dreams during both non-REM sleep and REM sleep, but the latter are the ones you are most likely to remember. They tend to be more vivid, more likely to have a narrative, and more likely to involve emotive, strange, or unsettling events and scenarios. Most people dream about five times during each eight-hour period of sleep, meaning that you have about 1,825 dreams each year.

What are dreams for?

The purpose and meaning of dreams, if any, has attracted the interest of philosophers and artists throughout history. There are three main theories:

- Dreams are the imaginary acting out of repressed and unconscious desires, represented symbolically. This theory was first proposed by Freud, and developed much further by Jung, who theorized that during dreams we encounter archetypes—symbols that are common to every subconscious mind. In interacting with these archetypes, we are encountering forces of nature. Both Freud and Jung saw dreams as a great opportunity for insight into the psyche.
- Dreams represent conscious concerns, fears, hopes, and anxieties, but transformed into different images. This theory is related to Freud's but is a lot

more straightforward. Again, the implication is that by exploring your dreams you can learn about your psyche.

- Dreams are a way of going over information gathered during the day, filtering out junk, selecting and rehearsing the important stuff, and integrating it with instincts and knowledge already present. Dreams are essential for learning, especially for the developing mind of an infant, which might explain why newborn babies spend up to 70 percent of their sleep time in REM sleep.

Can dreams help you?

Apart from offering potential insights into your conscious and subconscious mind, there is also the intriguing possibility that dreams provide a forum for enhanced creativity. Several prominent scientists report stories of how they struggled with a seemingly intractable problem, only to dream the solution. The story of Kekule, discoverer of the structure of benzene (at the time a difficult question in chemistry), is a classic example. He nodded off pondering on the problem, and dreamed of a snake swallowing its own tail. On awaking, the circular image led him to realize that a ring structure explained the strange chemistry of benzene.

Sleep patterns

Your lifestyle has a major impact on your sleep schedule, determining how many hours of sleep you get and also the quality of that sleep. Sleep is extremely important for memory. We still don't know exactly what sleep is for, but one of the main theories is that it provides a period of conscious inactivity during which the brain can get on with mental "housekeeping" tasks—in particular, memory "housekeeping." According to Dr. Karim Nader at McGill University in Montreal, "Sleep helps some memories 'mature' and also prunes out unimportant memories."

During the day a lot of memories, some important and others dispensable, build up in an intermediate-memory "cache," where memories start to undergo the process of encoding for long-term storage. The "housekeeping" theory of sleep says that it is only during sleep that the wheat can be sorted from the chaff, as it were, with the brain discarding dispensable memories to make room for the important material to be consolidated.

For this process to work properly, however, you need to get sufficient sleep—the amount differs from person to person, but for most people it's around seven to eight hours. Quality of sleep also matters. Many factors can affect this. Alcohol, drugs, caffeine, smoking, or stress can cause interrupted slumber, which doesn't provide enough of the truly refreshing deep sleep.

In the 1990s there was a flurry of excitement over research that seemed to show that simply playing classical music—especially Mozart—to children could boost their intellectual performance, including their memory abilities. As a result, children across the world were bombarded with Mozart at school, at home, and even while still in the womb. In Georgia (U.S.), public funds were allocated to the production and distribution of a classical-music CD to all new mothers in the state.

Unfortunately, the hype turned out to be ill-founded. The original research upon which the claims were based was actually performed on college students, not children, and it involved just a small sample of subjects, who showed transient intellectual improvements. These effects may simply have been caused by increased concentration or relaxation linked to the music. Follow-up research has indicated that classical music produces no specific intellectual benefits, but some studies suggest that classical music calms children and helps them to concentrate. If you want to boost your child's memory abilities through music, it seems there is no shortcut—proper training in an instrument can help, but simply putting on a record won't.

Relaxation and the brain

Sleep is not the only restorative process available to you. Everybody needs rest time during waking hours in order to recharge batteries. Crucially, this does not mean a period simply of physical inactivity, but of mental respite. In the modern world, this is increasingly rare, as time is filled with work, travel, or watching television. (Many people talk of "relaxing in front of the TV," but this is one of the great misconceptions of modern life—watching TV is a form of mental stimulation, not relaxation.)

The benefits of relaxation

Making time to practice relaxation techniques can produce physiological, psychological, and emotional benefits. High blood pressure and cardiovascular problems have both been linked to stress. Relaxation can help to prevent, lower, or improve both. It also helps prevent irritability and mood swings, aids concentration, memory, and learning, and can even help with mental illness. Use the relaxation cards to guide your program. Start with the breathing exercises on the cards, as this skill is central to effective relaxation.

Go to page 177 for a series of exercises to test and improve your relaxation techniques.

Nutrition and Lifestyle

All the mental training and honing in the world won't do you much good if you don't make sure your brain gets the nutrients it needs, while protecting it from the slings and arrows of outrageous lifestyle habits. Diet and lifestyle lay the foundations for optimum brain health, and therefore optimum mental functioning. The old adage "you are what you eat" certainly applies to the brain, which means that diet plays a surprisingly significant role in your mental life so unless you give yourself the right dietary and lifestyle platform, you won't be able to make the most of your intellectual gifts.

Feed your mind

We often hear talk of brain food, but what does this really mean? Your brain needs all the same food groups as the rest of your body, but there are some particular nutrients and foodstuffs that are necessary for optimal brain health, and in which the average diet is deficient. This section outlines the main types of nutrient that you need. To learn where to find them, see the Macronutrient and Micronutrient Challenge cards.

The main food groups

The main three types of macronutrients are protein, carbohydrate, and fat.

- **Protein**: The diets of most people in the Western world include an excess of protein, but even so, we often risk missing out on some vital ones. Proteins are made up of subunits called amino acids, which come in 20 different varieties. Your body can synthesize most of these for itself, but there are eight that must be obtained from your diet. The best way to ensure that you get all of these is to eat a variety of protein foods—this is particularly important for vegetarians.

- **Carbohydrate**: The brain accounts for just 2 percent of your body weight, but uses up 30 percent of your daily calorie intake! It's an energy-hungry organ that needs constant fueling, so skipping meals can result in impaired mental function. This is especially true of breakfast, when your brain needs fresh energy sources to help it tool up for the day, yet unfortunately this is the most commonly missed meal. Research shows that for both children and adults, missing breakfast impairs concentration, learning, and memory, and makes you unhappy, irritable, and lethargic.

Most of the fuel you need is provided by carbohydrates, but all carbohydrates are not the same. Simple carbs are those that consist of mainly sugars or are heavily processed, such as white flour (or anything made with it), candy, chocolate, cakes, potato chips, soda, and most breakfast cereals. Complex carbs tend to come from less processed foods, such as wholewheat bread or pasta, brown rice, unprocessed cereal, legumes (pulses), and vegetables.

Simple carbs are quickly broken down in the digestive tract and absorbed into the bloodstream, providing a rapid elevation of blood-sugar levels and a "sugar rush" effect. After the sugar rush comes a rapid drop-off, which can leave you feeling groggy and irritable, with negative effects on memory performance.

The question of supplements

Supplements seem to offer a handy shortcut to optimum nutrition—simply pop an A–Z multivitamin in your mouth and you're done. There are, however, arguments for and against them. Most modern diets are deficient, if only minimally, in many micronutrients, although the level of deficiency in the general population is the subject of fierce debate. Also, modern agricultural methods have led to soil degradation, which in turn lowers the nutrient content of the food we eat. The solution would seem to be to take supplements.

On the other hand, not only are many doctors skeptical about the true level of deficiencies, but also there is doubt about how good supplements are at actually getting micronutrients into the bloodstream in useful forms. When you take a vitamin pill, for instance, most of the vitamin is either never absorbed by your gut or is quickly flushed out of the blood by your kidneys. There is even evidence that in certain circumstances some supplements can be harmful.

On balance, the answer seems to be to make sparing use of supplements, while improving your diet. Micronutrients consumed in wholefood form, rather than as supplements, are absorbed more efficiently and are more likely to arrive in the bloodstream in a form that is useful to your system. They are also unlikely to be harmful.

All this disturbs your natural patterns of alertness, causing rapid swings between drowsiness and hyperactivity, which is not conducive to concentration or memory performance.

Complex carbs, on the other hand, are broken down slowly in the digestive tract, releasing a steady trickle of fuel into the bloodstream. This helps maintain an even level of alertness for long periods of time, which aids both learning and recall.

Optimal memory performance, therefore, is best served by eating complex carbohydrates and avoiding simple ones. This is particularly important at the beginning of the day. After a long period without food, your body needs fuel, and numerous studies have shown that skipping breakfast has negative consequences for mental performance, including memory, in both children and adults. However, eating something sweet, such as a bun or a highly processed and sugary breakfast cereal (which is almost every brand of cereal you will find in the grocery store, including those that profess to be healthy), will simply flood your system with a short-lived sugar rush. Memory performance will benefit much more from a breakfast of complex carbohydrates, such as wholewheat toast, a banana, or unprocessed wholegrain cereal. However, the same foods can cause drowsiness if eaten at lunchtime, so make your lunches protein-rich and low in carbohydrates and fat.

- **Fat**: Not all fat is bad, and the brain is particularly hungry for a type of fat called essential fatty acids (EFAs)—in fact, most people don't get enough of these. So while you should seek to lower your intake of saturated fat (found in oils that have been heated, such as those used for frying, fried foods, red meat, junk food, butter, cheese, cakes, potato chips, etc.), you almost certainly need to increase your EFA intake.

Micronutrients for memory

Vitamins and minerals are absolutely essential to the healthy functioning of your body and mind. Usually all that is necessary is to avoid a dietary deficiency of each micronutrient, but sometimes getting extra can give your memory power a boost. The list overleaf includes the most important memory micronutrients and where you can find them.

- **Beta-carotene**: This is a pro-vitamin (it is transformed in the body into vitamin A) that is found in colorful or dark green fruits and vegetables, such as peppers, spinach, apricots, and pumpkin. There is evidence that beta-carotene deficiency impairs mental performance, including memory. Smokers should avoid beta-carotene supplements, and this is one micronutrient that you should definitely try to get from your diet.

- **B vitamins**: The B-group is a large family of vitamins with many roles, one of which is maintaining good memory function. Thiamine, found in wholegrains, pork and liver, brewer's yeast, soybeans, peanuts, and dried beans, is essential to memory function. Deficiency causes memory problems and can eventually lead to permanent damage. Riboflavin, niacin, B6, and B12 are other B vitamins in which a deficiency can cause memory problems. Good sources are wholegrains, meat (especially organ meats), beans, and peanuts. There is some evidence that boosting your intake of the B-vitamin choline—found in lecithin, which itself is found in egg yolks and soybeans—can help to slow age-related memory decline.

- **Magnesium**: Magnesium is an important micronutrient, but most adults eat less than the recommended 400mg a day. According to a recent study, one of the roles played by magnesium is to regulate a brain receptor that is vital in learning and memory, so you may need to boost your magnesium intake to ensure optimal memory function. There is even some evidence that increased magnesium intake may help reverse memory loss and improve recall in middle age. Foods rich in it include dark green leafy vegetables, brown rice, sunflower seeds, peas, and beans.

- **Zinc**: Zinc deficiency can impair short-term memory and attention, and is surprisingly common. Good sources of zinc include oysters, extra-lean meats, poultry, fish, organ meats, dairy products and eggs, wholegrains, wheatgerm, black-eyed peas, beans, nuts, seeds, and fermented soybean paste (miso).

- **Iron**: This is the essential ingredient of hemoglobin, the oxygen-carrying molecule in the blood, and therefore plays a vital role in keeping the brain supplied with enough oxygen to function at optimum levels. It also has a direct role in brain function in childhood and adulthood. Deficiency causes fatigue, poor attention, and impaired memory. Good sources include meat (especially organ meats), sardines, egg yolks, and dark green leafy vegetables such as spinach and kale.

- **EFAs**: Strictly speaking, essential fatty acids belong to the macronutrient

Inside the brain: fighting free radicals

One of the major roles of micronutrients is to act as antioxidants. In normal functioning, cells generate highly reactive molecules called free radicals, which can damage cell machinery and DNA. Extra free radicals are formed by exposure to sunlight, smoking, toxins in food, and so on. To mop up these free radicals, and thus limit the damage they can do, cells use antioxidants. Free radicals are responsible for much of the wear and tear that affects nerve cells in the brain, reducing the ability to form new memories, maintain old ones, and access those in storage. Antioxidants help prevent this damage, thus protecting your memory abilities. This is one reason that micronutrients are good for your memory.

food group oils and fats, but they are often treated as micronutrients because there are similar issues of deficiency in the diet of the general population. EFAs are especially important for building and maintaining healthy nerve cells, and thus for optimum memory performance. Good sources include oily fish, such as tuna, sardines, mackerel, and salmon (which is the reason that fish has sometimes been called "brain food"), and seeds and the oils that come from them, such as hemp seeds, rapeseed oil, sunflower oil, and evening primrose oil. Try sprinkling seeds onto cereal and salads or adding them to bread dough.

- **Folic acid (or folate)**: Deficiency can cause fetal developmental disorders and, in adults, impaired cognitive function, depression, and dementia.
- **Calcium**: Needed for nerve signaling. Deficiency can cause muscle twitching and fatigue.
- **Potassium**: Also involved in nerve signaling. Deficiency can cause apathy and weakness.

Exercises and strategies to try

Macronutrient challenge

- Proteins: Most people eat far more than their daily requirements of protein, but for proper brain function you need to be careful to combine different sources of protein. Make sure your protein sources include some foods from this list: legumes (beans, lentils, peas), soy beans, nuts, fish. By varying your protein sources, you can be sure that you get all the essential amino acids that your body can't make for itself.

- Carbohydrates: Try to make sure the bulk of your carbohydrate intake comes from sources of complex carbohydrates: wholewheat pasta, wholewheat bread, unprocessed potatoes (or other starchy root vegetables, e.g., yams), brown rice, fruit, breakfast cereals, legumes.

- Fats: Cut down on saturated fats, and boost your intake of the following sources of essential fatty acids: salmon, tuna, mackerel, herring, sardines, trout, anchovies, canola oil, olive oil, sunflower oil, evening primrose oil. (Heating oils breaks down their healthy properties.)

Pre-test meals

For optimal mental performance during a test, you need a fast supply of energy to the brain, but this should not, at the same time, produce a sudden, massive rise in blood sugar, which can be debilitating. You also want to avoid heavy, fat-laden dishes that lie in your gut and divert blood away from the brain. Try these:

- Pasta with tomato-based sauce
- Rice with beans and steamed vegetables
- Baked potatoes with baked beans
- Wholewheat bread and vegetable soup
- Couscous or steamed wheat grains with beans and steamed vegetables

All portions should be small to medium size.

Work Out, Stay Sharp

Contrary to popular prejudice, brain and brawn are linked—in several ways. Mental performance depends on brain function, which depends on a healthy blood supply to the brain, which in turn depends on a healthy cardiovascular system. Aerobic exercise is the best way to maintain this, helping keep the arteries clear, blood pressure low, the heart strong, and the blood pumping to the brain. If you're feeling groggy and are struggling to clear your mind and recall something, you could do worse than go for a run, a swim, or try some other form of aerobic activity.

Put your IQ to work

IQ scores do relate to the real world. IQ is a powerful predictor of real-world outcomes such as earning power, job success, and staying out of debt, which in turn tells us that intelligence is an important factor in all these areas of life. This is hardly a revelation, but it shows that it pays to maximize your potential brainpower—applying your intelligence to its fullest potential at work and at home could reap real rewards. At the same time, you will be exercising the skills you need in order to do well on an IQ test.

Improve your performance at work

Many of the intellectual skills that you will practice and hone by working through the questions, tests, and exercises in this pack will stand you in good stead at work, in the following ways:

Focus: What attracts many people to puzzles and quizzes is the way they engage the mind to the exclusion of all else. When you are absorbed in a puzzle, your attention is

Head

Studies on rats suggest that exercise is linked to elevated levels of nerve growth factor. This is a type of hormone that boosts the development of strong networks between nerve cells and encourages them to form synaptic connections—yet another example of how fitness benefits brain functioning.

entirely focused. Not only is this quite relaxing in some ways, but it is also a powerful tool for intellectual achievement. Transferring this intensity of focus or ability to concentrate to a work environment would be extremely helpful, increasing your efficiency and productivity. The advantage of regular practice of IQ-style brain-teasers is that it teaches you to focus your mind on the task at hand and trains you in the art of shutting out mental distractions.

Verbal ability: Practicing tests of verbal aptitude sharpens your verbal skills, teaches you new vocabulary and new word relations, and hones your ability to make links between words and use words in new ways. These are all useful skills at work, particularly for preparing presentations, writing reports, or simply getting your ideas across. Make the process work both ways by using your daily encounters with language to push your verbal abilities—for example, look up new or unfamiliar words and make an effort to remember them.

Numerical ability: Many people are math-phobic, which is a form of learned helplessness, but training with numerical questions can both sharpen mathematical skills and increase familiarity, and therefore comfort levels, with this type of material. By the same token, working with figures and doing math at the office should boost your

ability with numerical–mathematical questions in an IQ test. More generally, the thinking processes that help people to solve math problems successfully include clear analysis and statement of problems, and logical and creative thinking toward a solution—all qualities that would be helpful at work.

Logical thinking: Logical thinking, which includes critical-thinking skills, is actually not widely practiced in the real world. Yet becoming more familiar with the basics of logical and critical thinking could make you more effective at constructing arguments and investigating proposals. It is particularly important for managers and engineers to avoid errors of reasoning that could lead to flaws in their plans or systems. Everyday life is the best place to encounter fallacies and poor logic, and becoming more aware of these in daily life could boost your logic skills and thus your performance on tests.

Visuospatial ability: This is particularly useful in some specific walks of life, such as design, art, or architecture. But exercising your visuospatial abilities could also benefit you in an everyday office situation, making you better at creating, handling, and interpreting graphs, charts, plans, diagrams, and presentations in general. More abstractly, it might help you to form graphic concepts of nonvisual material, such as when visualizing a process or system. Greater familiarity with such material in your daily life could also help you to answer related questions more successfully in an IQ-style test—for example, people who work with, say, diagrams or with engine blocks in their daily lives are probably better equipped to solve visuospatial problems.

Creative thinking: Creativity is a buzzword in business and management circles these days, and more value is being attached to creativity in the workplace. Whether practicing IQ tests can enhance creativity directly is uncertain, but if it gets you into the habit of employing bursts of inspiration or thinking out of the box, it could well benefit you at work. In particular, it could help you to contribute more and better ideas in meetings and impress your colleagues and superiors with new ways of looking at things or fresh approaches to getting things done.

Get the most out of training and research

Many of the benefits just described could also apply to the more specific areas of learning, training, and research. Concentration is essential for efficient, productive research, and verbal, numerical, and visuospatial ability can help you to better understand and remember related material. Logical thinking can help you to identify core arguments and critically evaluate the claims, assumptions, evidence, and conclusions that are involved. One could also argue that memory skills benefit from mental training, and these in turn will help you to learn.

The windmills of your mind

More generally, training and research are related to crystallized intelligence and the evidence is that this is partly dependent on fluid intelligence. One analogy describes fluid intelligence as the machinery in your mental factory, and crystallized intelligence as the stored products of that machinery. By practicing IQ-test material you are hopefully sharpening and maximizing your fluid capabilities, so this should have knock-on benefits when it comes to building up a store of crystallized intelligence through learning or research.

The intelligent household

Mental exercise needn't be restricted to the workplace, of course. You can incorporate it into your domestic life as well, to help keep you mentally sharp, hone your abilities in several different areas, and increase your familiarity with and command of the skills you need to succeed in IQ tests. Here are a few strategies you could try, which might at least give you a jumping-off point for devising your own ways of working mental exercise into your domestic routine.

Out with lists—in with memory games

Normally people use physical aide-mémoires, such as shopping or to-do lists, to compensate for the frailties of their own memories. Instead, you could try making a conscious effort to use mnemonic strategies and tricks to remember lists. The point of this sort of exercise is to hone your memory powers, which can benefit the abilities tested by IQ-style questions.

Visual memory cues

- Memorize a shopping list by visualizing a fairytale-style story of linked events featuring the items on your list. The more outlandish the images, the more likely you are to remember the list.

- Use features of the domestic environment as cues to trigger associated memories. (Need to remember a birthday? Visualize a striking and memorable image such as the birthday boy springing out from a giant birthday cake blocking the front door, and singing "Happy Birthday, Mr President.")

Mental arithmetic for the home

Housekeeping can involve a surprising amount of mental arithmetic. Many people avoid this, but you should embrace it as an opportunity to exercise your numerical–mathematical faculties. Avoid using a calculator (unless it's to check your answers later) when working out home budgets and bills. To boost your working memory, don't use a pen or paper when adding or subtracting—try doing them exclusively in your head.

$$2 \times 9 \qquad 67 + 174 \qquad 43 - 37 \qquad 18 \div 3$$

The enriched environment

Developmental psychologists say that the best way to ensure that children achieve their maximum intellectual potential (including IQ score) is to bring them up in a rich and intellectually challenging environment. If you have children, therefore, you should aim to provide as much intellectual and sensory stimulation for them as you can from the earliest age possible (although the stimulation  needs to be age-appropriate). Adults can also benefit from environments like this, because the evidence shows that mental stimulation helps to prevent or slow down cognitive decline.

Keep your brain young

A lot of people today are thinking about the effects of aging on their gray matter: what psychologists call age-related cognitive decline. One reason this has become a major issue is that demographic changes—sometimes termed "the graying of society"—mean that more people are living for longer. Another reason, however, is that there is an increasing awareness that age-related cognitive decline is not inevitable, that it can be actively delayed or prevented, and that it is within the power of the individual to take this action. This section discusses these issues and includes some of the lifestyle strategies that could help you to maximize your IQ score now as well as prevent it from declining as you become older.

Intelligence and age

IQ scores remain pretty much stable throughout adulthood and into old age, contrary to the popular image of old age as a decline into dotage. In fact, if you test someone as a child and then give them the same test with the same marking system 70 years later, chances are that their score will go up by several points. Such an increase could be linked to the idea that crystallized intelligence improves with age, as you build up a store of knowledge and experience. (This includes information as well as skills and ways of thinking about and doing things.) On the other hand, most studies show that fluid intelligence and mental speed (which may be very nearly the same thing) tend to decline with age. Since mental speed is strongly linked to g—the general intelligence factor that underlies all the other sub-categories of intelligence—does this mean that you inevitably lose g as you age?

The Mankato nuns

One famous study shows that it is possible to retain mental sharpness into extreme old age. In the Mankato Nun Study, a group of elderly nuns from the convent of the School Sisters of Notre Dame on Good Counsel Hill in Mankato, Minnesota, underwent a variety of tests, and also comparisons with material they had produced when they were much younger. Many of the nuns had reached ripe old ages—some were over 100. What the research showed, among other things, was that it is possible to maintain mental agility and sharpness up to and beyond the age of 100. Many of the elderly nuns scored just as high as ever in tests and displayed their mental acuity in their daily lives, through their learning, teaching, reading, debating, and mentally challenging leisure pursuits such as crosswords and other puzzles.

Staying sharp

Studies like the Mankato Nun Study have suggested a range of strategies for keeping your mental faculties sharp. The overall message is to do as the nuns do: challenge yourself with crosswords, puzzles, jigsaws, reading, education (such as learning a new language), new pastimes and hobbies, keeping a journal, or practicing "domestic math" (see page 120). Rather than simply vegging out in front of the TV, keep your brain ticking.

Rush of blood to the head

Why should challenging mental activity prove so effective at keeping your brain sharp? One clue comes from a study by the neurologist John Stirling Meyer of the Baylor College of Medicine. He showed that people of post-retirement age who kept working or pursued new interests maintained a healthy cerebral blood flow, whereas those who didn't showed significant decline in the amount of blood getting to the brain.

This is where IQ-style tests, questions, and exercises, like the ones in this pack, come in. Working through the questions and challenges in the cards and workbook provides an excellent mental workout, and making a habit of exercising your mental abilities in this fashion could thus benefit both your performance on IQ tests and your long-term cognitive health.

Maintain your brain

Mental exercise of the sort described above is only one aspect of brain maintenance. More physical measures, including dietary and lifestyle factors, can also help to prevent cognitive decline. (This may not be the same as boosting your IQ, but it can certainly prevent it from going down.) What is particularly important with regard to IQ is that these are the same factors that, on a short-term basis, can have a significant influence on your IQ score, depending on a range of lifestyle factors—the same ones that are important for general brain maintenance.

Exercise

Aerobic exercise boosts circulation and cardiovascular health, which in turn benefits the brain through ensuring a healthy blood supply. In fact, according to Waneen Spirduso, director of the Institute of Gerontology at the University of Texas at Austin, there are two factors that best predict an older person's performance on tests of mental agility. These are the number of years the person has exercised in the past and the person's current aerobic capacity.

A major study in Wisconsin, the Wisconsin Registry for Alzheimer's Prevention, has shown that even mild exercise, like a regular walk, can boost mental performance— seniors who walk regularly score better and maintain cognitive powers for longer than those who don't. The farther they walked, the better their brains were.

As regards IQ tests, exercise is important both for its general brain-health benefits and because it is a major factor in the related area of sleep, energy levels, stress reduction, and relaxation.

Energy levels

Taking an IQ test is similar to taking any other type of exam, in that your performance on the day is what counts. This can be affected by lots of factors that have little to do with your intelligence. Particularly important are issues of alertness and energy levels, which in turn

depend on sleep, daily rhythms, stress levels, and diet and fitness. All of these issues are also important for brain maintenance. Get your alertness, energy, relaxation, and focus levels right and it could make a difference of 5 IQ points or more to your performance.

Low-energy scenario

You will perform worse on an IQ test if you are tired or stressed, which could be linked to:

• Insufficient or poor-quality sleep.

- Mental, physical, or emotional stress.

- Being unfit.

- Skipping meals or eating the wrong sorts of foods, such as stodgy, fatty foods that lead to drowsiness, or sugary or highly processed foods that are responsible for swings in blood-sugar levels, which in turn can cause swings in mental alertness. Hence the infamous, short-lived sugar-high followed by an extended "crash."

- The time of day. Your brain follows a 90-minute cycle of high and low alertness, while over the course of the day your whole body is responsive to  what are called circadian rhythms. Different people have slightly different rhythms. Some people are "early birds" or "larks," who naturally wake up early and are energetic, focused, and alert in the morning, while others are "night owls," who naturally wake up late and are at their best in the evening. Take a test at the wrong time and you could be out of synch with your body clock.

- Alcohol, caffeine, nicotine, and recreational drugs have mostly negative effects on alertness and energy levels. Some, like caffeine and nicotine, can temporarily increase alertness levels, but they may also make it harder to concentrate and they often have a "come-down" or "payback" period. All of them can disrupt sleep patterns, with spiraling effects.

High-energy scenario

You will be well placed to perform to your maximum potential in an IQ test if you are fit, well rested, relaxed, and calm as a result of the following:

- You've had plenty of undisturbed, high-quality sleep.

- You've eaten a suitable meal such as a breakfast of slow-release carbohydrate sources (for example, fruit and wholegrain, unprocessed cereal or toast) and have avoided alcohol, caffeine, and drugs.

- You've factored in your own personal body clock by arranging to take the test at the time of day when you know you'll be at your best—or, when this is not possible, you've compensated by doing everything else right.

Does last-minute cramming ever work?

If you're faced with a big exam, the obvious temptation is to study up to the last minute possible, even if this means skipping a few hours of sleep the night before. Resist the temptation because it is likely to be counterproductive.

• Tiredness affects mental abilities such as memory and concentration, so during the night, encoding (i.e., learning) will be more difficult, while the next day recall will be harder (not to mention the effects of fatigue on intellectual performance).

• Without a full night's sleep, the memories you are trying to lay down will not go through the consolidation process offered by the mental "housekeeping" of sleep.

• By disrupting your sleeping patterns you are also unlikely to be eating properly. You may have drunk caffeine and eaten junk food in place of slow-release carbohydrates.

There is simply no substitute for study carried out over a suitably long period—if you've left it to the last minute, an all-night cramming session is unlikely to help.

Familiarity breeds calm

Stress has come up several times in this book—it can be a negative factor in both the long and short term. In the long term, stress is implicated in cardiovascular health problems. In the short term, although a little stress (the amount depends on what sort of person you are) can boost performance, on the whole it is counter-productive, makes it hard to concentrate, and is mentally exhausting. This is unfortunate, because for many people a natural consequence of taking an IQ test or doing any sort of timed test is to feel stressed. Some people become extremely agitated under exam-style pressure.

This is where practice on IQ-style material can come in very useful. The more you familiarize yourself with the types, formats, and content of questions, the more relaxed you will be in the buildup to a test, and the less stressed you will be when you see the actual questions. This applies even to the questions you'd normally throw up your hands in despair over (i.e., the mathematical questions). Calmness will make it easier to concentrate and could make a difference to your score.

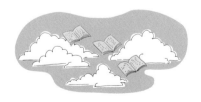

Part Four

Challenges & Exercises

Working Through the Tests and Challenges

Use the tests, brainteasers, and quizzes on the following pages to check your progress as you increase your brain power and develop your memory skills. Each section corresponds with a chapter in the book and the questions have been specifically designed to test and improve the areas covered, so whether you feel you want to enlarge your long-term memory or increase your score on IQ tests, there is a section to help you. As you work through each question, either write the answers in the space provided on the page or use a separate piece of paper—which will also allow you to return to the question at a later date to see how you have improved. After you have finished each test, turn to the answers on pages 179–189 to confirm how well you did, or find out where you went wrong.

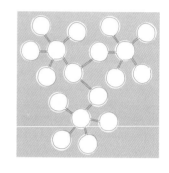

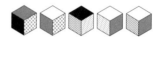

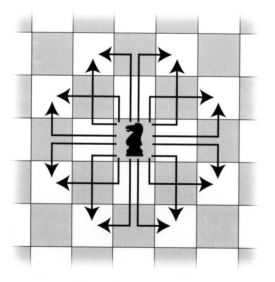

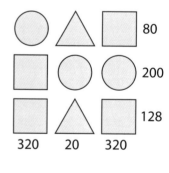

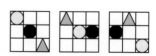

How You Think

How Are You Wired?

Assess your strengths and weaknesses

Before you start looking at the different areas in which you can improve your brain power do the following questionaire. For each of the questions below, select the answer that most honestly reflects your feelings, opinions, responses, or experiences. The questions in this test are arranged in groups that correspond to different areas of mental ability, as shown in the book. Breaking down your score by group can help you identify your mental strengths and weaknesses (see page 179 for the scores).

Questions 1–5 look at intelligence as the ability measured by IQ tests. To find out more, look at the tests on "Intelligence and Forward Thinking" from page 132.

Questions 6–11 look at creative and lateral thinking. If you scored poorly in this area, to find out more, look at the tests on "Creativity and Lateral Thinking" from page 135.

Questions 12–14 look at communication abilities, including verbal and non-verbal communication skills. To find out more, read "Language and Communication" and study the tests from pages 140.

Questions 15–17 look at how good your memory is. To find out more, read "Memory and Concentration" and look at the related tests from page 158.

Questions 18–20 look at your ability to relax and your knowledge about sleep, stress, and relaxation. To find out more, read "Sleeping and Relaxation"; see the exercises on page 177.

Questions 21–23 look at issues of diet and lifestyle, and how these affect your mental abilities. To find out more, read the section on "Nutrition and Lifestyle."

1   How do you feel when your friends are discussing something involving politics or science?
a) They don't know half as much as you.
b) Embarrassed because you can't follow the conversation.
c) Interested because they're making good points.

2   Somebody from the tech department at work is giving a seminar on the new office computer system to your team. You've never worked with a system like this before. How do you feel?
a) This stuff is way too complicated—and you've never been good with computers.
b) You'll probably be all right once you've had a chance to practice.
c) No problem—most systems work on the same principles, so you should have no trouble picking this one up.

3   *What do you think of television news programs these days?*
a) They've been dumbed down to the point of being unwatchable.
b) They're too complicated to follow.
c) Most are at about the right level.

4   *The restaurant, 11:30 Friday night. The check's just arrived and it's time to figure out who owes what. Who gets to do the job?*
a) If someone's got a calculator handy, you'll take on the challenge.
b) You always get the job because you can do the math in your head.
c) Not you in a million years—unless they want to be there all night!

5   *You and a friend are driving to another town. It's your job to navigate. Are you:*
a) The best navigator since Captain Cook?
b) OK, but you have to turn the map around when you're going south?
c) Hopeless—you couldn't find your way to the neighborhood store?

6   *You're taking part in a brainstorming session at work. How do you perform?*
a) You come up with a dozen ideas to most people's one.
b) It seems like a waste of time, and you don't really understand it.
c) You can hold your own.

7   *What's your attitude to a challenging crossword?*
a) Bring it on!
b) You'll give it a try, but those clues sure are hard.
c) You wouldn't know where to start— best to stick to simpler ones.

8   *You have to do some emergency plumbing to clear the drain, but don't*
have a sink plunger. What would you be most likely to do?
a) Wait until you can get hold of a plunger.
b) Try to clear the drain some other way.
c) Fashion a makeshift plunger using half a tennis ball and a broom handle.

9   *Which of the statements about you and your partner is most accurate?*
a) You always know if he/she is upset about something.
b) His/her moods are a mystery to you.
c) You can tell when he/she is upset, but you usually have to ask why.

10 *The woman next to you at work looks like she's been crying. What do you do?*
a) Leave her to her own devices.
b) Alert your boss.
c) Discreetly invite her to step out for a coffee break, and then ask her if she wants to talk about anything.

11 *If you had a problem, how would you handle it?*
a) Hope it went away.
b) Stew over it until you came up with a solution.
c) Find someone to talk it over with.

12 *Someone uses a clever putdown against you. How do you react?*
a) Dispatch them with a cutting riposte of devastating wit.
b) Give them a piece of your mind.
c) Think of the perfect response about an hour later.

13 *You're at a party and you've got your eye on a good-looking person on the other side of the room. What are you like at feeling "the vibes"?*
a) You can always tell whether someone's interested from the way they stand.

b) If you can make eye contact you'll know whether it's worth a shot.

c) You never seem to be able to judge this until it's too late and you've completely missed your chance.

14 *You've got a big job interview. What's the first thing you do when you walk in the room?*
a) Take the seat that's offered you.
b) Look the interviewer in the eye and give him/her a firm handshake.
c) Find somewhere for your bag and coat.

15 *Which of the following best describes you preparing to leave the house?*
a) Desperately hunting for your keys and billfold.
b) Forgetting your keys and billfold altogether.
c) Finding your keys and billfold right where you always leave them.

16 *You've been at a party for a couple of hours and find yourself talking to the person you were introduced to when you came in. Do you:*
a) Remember his name and what he does?
b) Have to search for his name for a few seconds?
c) Have no recollection of his name or job?

17 *When you go shopping, do you:*
a) Have to write a list?
b) Remember what you need without a list?
c) Write a list, but forget to take it with you?

18 *You've got a big meeting on Monday. How do you spend the weekend?*
a) Stay in bed really late on Saturday and Sunday, to pay off your sleep debt from the previous week.
b) Stay out late on Friday and Saturday—and catch up on sleep on Sunday.

c) Get up at the usual time on Saturday and Sunday, but make sure that you get to bed nice and early on both days.

19 *How do you feel about your dreams?*
a) You can never remember them.
b) They're weird and sometimes funny.
c) They're worth recording because sometimes you find unexpected solutions to the previous day's problems in them.

20 *Work keeps piling up on your desk, you've got deadlines tomorrow, and you have to give a presentation this afternoon. What do you do at lunchtime?*
a) Make sure you get away from your desk and go outside for lunch, even if it's only for half an hour.
b) Work through lunch.
c) Eat a sandwich at your desk.

21 *What's your idea of good brain food?*
a) Multivitamin and mineral supplements.
b) A good fried meal.
c) A green salad with tuna, pine nuts, and pumpkin and sesame seeds.

22 *You've got an exam in the afternoon. What do you have to eat beforehand?*
a) Nothing—you're too nervous.
b) Pasta and a banana at lunchtime.
c) A candy bar just before you go in.

23 *Smoking:*
a) Stimulates the nervous system and sharpens the mind.
b) Doesn't affect your brain—it's the heart and lungs you've got to worry about.
c) Impairs brain function.

To find your scores and personal assessment, turn to page 179.

Intelligence and Forward Thinking

IQ-style test

The test below is based on the General Mental Abilities test devised by Louis Janda et al. in 1995. It looks at several different types of intelligence, including verbal, spatial, and mathematical abilities. Although this version of the test has not been validated with large numbers of subjects, it can give you a good idea of where you rate in the intelligence stakes, and which area you need to pay particular attention to.

The test is in multiple choice form. Take as long as you want. You can use a pencil and extra paper to work out the answers, but don't use a calculator or computer! The answers are on page 179.

Verbal abilities

Select the alternative that best completes the sentence.

1 *Enlarge is to expand
   as ascend is to* . . . .
   a) fall
   b) mount
   c) depress
   d) accumulate

2 *Intense is to concentrated
   as boring is to* . . . .
   a) profound
   b) deep
   c) substantial
   d) banal

3 *Examine is to ignore
   as pithy is to* . . . .
   a) short
   b) long-winded
   c) concise
   d) quick

4 *Vitriolic is to honeyed
   as aloof is to* . . . .
   a) snotty
   b) cold
   c) passionate
   d) uninterested

Select the word/phrase that comes closest in meaning to the initial word.

5 *Esoteric*
   a) obvious
   b) plain
   c) occult
   d) transcendent

6 *Mundane*
   a) quotidian
   b) unreal
   c) fabulous
   d) mythic

7 *Pathos*
   a) ridiculous
   b) hysterical
   c) tear-jerking
   d) melodramatic

Mathematical ability

8   If $6x + 3y = 12$, then $2x + y = ?$
   a) 4
   b) $\frac{1}{3}$
   c) 6
   d) 2

9   What is $\frac{2}{3} \times \frac{3}{5} \times \frac{5}{3}$?
   a) $\frac{18}{45}$
   b) 2
   c) $\frac{3}{4}$
   d) $\frac{2}{3}$

10   The tennis club has 60 members. 45 of them are women. What percentage of the club's members are men?
   a) 30 percent
   b) 22.5 percent
   c) 15 percent
   d) 25 percent

11   Which of the following is the smallest number?
   a) $\frac{15}{28}$
   b) $\frac{31}{60}$
   c) $\frac{76}{150}$
   d) $\frac{6}{10}$

12   The average of three single-digit numbers is 8. What is the smallest that one of the numbers can be?
   a) 0
   b) 1
   c) 4
   d) 6

13   There are 64 players in a chess tournament where each match is a knockout match. How many matches are there overall?
   a) 32
   b) 63
   c) 64
   d) 128

14   Charlie is two years older than his dog. Eight years ago, Charlie was twice as old as his dog. How old is Charlie?
   a) 10
   b) 12
   c) 64
   d) 128

Spatial ability

15: Below is a pattern of a flattened cube. Using mental imagery, work out which of the cubes on the right cannot be created from the pattern.

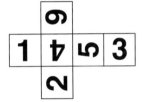

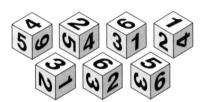

16: The squares below vary in size. How many sizes of square are there?

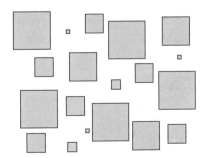

Brainstormers

Stopwatch challenge

Develop your mental timekeeping ability, powers of concentration, and general mental acuity with this simple task. For this challenge, you need a watch or clock with an analog second hand or digital seconds readout.

Look at the watch or clock, starting at the 12 o'clock position, or 00 seconds, and concentrate on it for 60 seconds. Then close your eyes and see if you can mentally time a minute. Open your eyes, and check the actual seconds that have passed. Keep practicing until you can time exactly a minute with your eyes closed.

Teleportation challenge

Develop your spatial reasoning ability by finding a place on a map and imagining what you would see if you were standing there, using the data on the map. Use any detailed map, and pick a spot at random, then visualize yourself on that spot and sketch the 360-degree panorama that would be visible to you. Start off with a map of an area familiar to you, and graduate to unfamiliar areas.

For a real challenge, pick a spot with complex natural features.

Navigation challenge

Develop your spatial reasoning abilities by locating a distant place on a map of your area. Look out the window and pick a distant spot that is just about visible. Then find it on a local map. Consider walking there at lunchtime, or on a free day, to check if you were right.

Before you set off, try to match features that you can see around your chosen spot to features on the map, and also try to use the information on the map to develop a mental picture of what you will see when you reach the spot. Check to see how well the reality matches up to your powers of visualization.

Upside-down mouse

Develop your spatial acuity and hand-eye coordination (which is controlled by the cerebellum, a kind of mini-brain that sits at the base of your brain). Next time you use a computer, turn the mouse the wrong way around on its mat—so that the part normally covered by the palm of your hand is now operated by the fingers, and vice versa.

With the mouse "upside down," the on-screen cursor movements are now controlled by the reverse of your normal actions—i.e., you have to move the mouse up to make the cursor go down, move right for left, etc. It's tricky, but it provides a good workout for the brain.

For an advanced challenge, use a drawing program and try to draw a picture using the upside-down mouse.

Creativity and Lateral Thinking

Creative problem-solving test

Test your creative thinking skills. To get an initial picture of your facility with creative and lateral thinking, the first test looks at your ability to find connections; then see if you can solve four classic puzzles. To answer the puzzles successfully, you'll need to think creatively about possible solutions or strategies for success. For each puzzle, record your thinking as far as you are able by making notes or documenting your efforts. The aim is not to time yourself or get a score, but to test how your thinking works. The answers are on page 180.

1   The remote associates test

For each of the three-word sets, come up with a fourth word that fits all of them. Allow yourself two minutes.

a) wet—ground—lash
b) animal—line—surprise
c) worm—shelf—telephone
d) group—power—pen
e) news—clip—wall
f) stick—even—maker
g) cloth—cottage—hard
h) lime—march—fire

2   The fox, corn, and chicken puzzle

Imagine that you are a farmer on one side of a river, who needs to ferry three things over to the other side: a fox, a chicken, and a bag of corn. There is only enough room in the boat for you and one of the three items at a time. While you are present they all behave, but the problem is that if you leave the fox alone with the chicken while you carry the corn, the fox will eat the chicken, and if you leave the chicken alone with the corn, the chicken will eat the corn. How can you get all three safely across to the other side?

3   The bus driver riddle

Imagine that you are a bus driver. The bus is empty to start with. At the first stop six men and four women get on. At the second stop one man and five women get on, and two men and two women get off. At the third stop seven men and five women get on, and four men and three women get off. At the fourth stop four men get on and three women get off. What is the bus driver's name?

4   *The nine-dot problem*

Connect the dots using just four straight lines without lifting your pencil/pen. The lines must pass through the center of each point.

5   *The messenger's problem*

Imagine you're a messenger who has to get a message to an army base that's six days' drive away, driving there in a truck. You've got plenty of gas at your home base, but a truck can carry just four cans of fuel—which is only enough to last for four days. Other trucks at the home base can accompany you. What's the minimum number of trucks you will need to ensure no one is left stranded between bases without any fuel?

Emotional intelligence–EQ-style test

This second test uses an inventory in conjunction with visual tests to give you an EI rating, or EQ score. Standardized testing for EQ is still a developing field, and there are no generally accepted testing tools as there are for IQ. This EQ test therefore provides only a guide to help you get a general picture of your EI abilities. The scoring is on page 181.

Inventory

For each item, choose the option that more accurately describes you.

1   a)   *My partner is often upset with me for no reason.*
b)   *I can always tell when my partner is about to cry.*

2   a)   *The opposite sex is a mystery to me.*
b)   *I can tell how a date is going after the first hour.*

3   a)   *Sentimental movies leave me cold.*
b)   *I'm a sucker for tearjerkers.*

4   a)   *I can make most people laugh.*
b)   *Other people rarely share my sense of humor.*

5   a)   *I can't be expected to know I've upset my partner if he/she won't explain what I've done wrong.*
b)   *When I exchange glances with my partner, I can tell exactly what he/she is thinking.*

6   a)   *I admire people who are blunt and forthright.*
b)   *I admire people who are tactful and diplomatic.*

7   a)   *I can tell when a girl/guy is giving me the cold shoulder.*
b)   *I wish people would just come out and say "no" when they mean "no."*

8   a)   *Many people are oversensitive.*
b)   *People should try to be more considerate of others.*

9 a) *I can read my boss like a book.*
   b) *I wish I knew what my boss wants from me.*

10 a) *When it comes to relationships, actions speak louder than words.*
   b) *It's not what you say, it's the way that you say it.*

11 a) *If someone at work is upset, I think it's best to just let them be.*
   b) *My friends know they can always talk to me about their problems.*

12 a) *I have trouble bringing up difficult subjects with people at work.*
   b) *If I asked for a raise I think I'd get one (assuming I deserved one).*

13 a) *I think I have learned something from each of my past relationships, even the ones that went wrong.*
   b) *When I make a mistake, I get really angry with myself.*

14 a) *After a hard day at work I shouldn't have to put up with my partner's complaints.*
   b) *I try to let my partner know that I don't take him/her for granted.*

Emotional understanding test

1 *Match the list of emotions to the pictures shown on page 138.*

Sadness	Anger
Happiness	Fear

2 *Two of your best friends are arguing over someone they both like. One has made a move and the other one doesn't think they should have. Now they're both upset; this could ruin their relationship! Should you get involved? What would you do?*

a) Stay out of it! If you stick your nose in you know you'll only make things worse.

b) Decide that they need their heads knocking together. You're going to tell them exactly what you think of them and how stupid they're being.

c) Try to talk to them individually and get them to consider things in the most calm and reasonable fashion they can manage. They might not agree with each other but at least you might get them to appreciate each other's point of view.

Brainstormers

Paper clip possibilities

The paper clip is widely considered to be a design classic because its form fits its function so completely. Yet a paperclip can have many other uses, if you are able to overcome its functional fixedness and think creatively—it could make a diving board for a flea, perhaps, or a button. For this exercise, engage in a daily brainstorming session where you pick an object and think up as many uses for it as possible.

Start with the paper clip and move on to other objects, animate or inanimate. The average number of uses a person can think up is 24—see if you can top that! Try this exercise with others to observe the dynamics of creativity in a group setting.

Find the similarities

For this exercise, you need to pick two things at random and brainstorm the ways in which they are similar. Some similarities will be obvious; others will require lateral thinking. For instance, if you picked a gas station and an orange, an obvious similarity might be that both contain the letter "g"; a less obvious similarity might be that both oranges and a gas station can fill you up.

Pick your own objects using the list below or an encyclopedia opened at random, and see how many similarities you can come up with—the average is 10.

15 objects to try:

Whale	Space shuttle
Candle	Broom
Photograph	Fingernail
Eraser	Skates
Lasso	Fork
Rose	Wig
Periscope	Grave
Feather	

Creative category challenge

Coming up with new ways to connect things is a valuable creative skill. This exercise challenges you to break out of a normal mind-set and invent new ways to categorize the familiar household items listed below.

Mixing bowl	Canned soup
Soap	Shampoo
Chair	Candle
Pillow	Matchbox
Spoon	Sugar
Books	Apple
Batteries	Pear
Eggs	Wine bottle
Walnuts	Cappuccino
Hamburger	Pot plant
Radio	Screwdriver
Milk	Pencil
Saucepan	Telephone

First write them out on a sheet of paper divided into obvious categories, such as perishables, canned goods, and toiletries, then rearrange them into new categories: edible v. inedible, packaged v. unpackaged, synthetic v. natural. Try to come up with increasingly lateral categories. How many can you devise?

Smile challenge

This simple exercise improves your Emotional Intelligence by boosting your abilities to be funny. Using humor is a large part of a healthy EI, and, in general, people who are good at telling jokes and making others laugh have well-developed EI.

Can you elicit a smile from others at will? It can be daunting, particularly with those you don't know well, so start by:

- Gauging the mood of others around you

- Suiting your humor to others' temperaments and interests

- Choosing a relaxed moment to introduce humor

Select three people and aim to make them smile or laugh at least once during the day. Begin with a friendly person, then someone more distant, and finish with a crabby colleague.

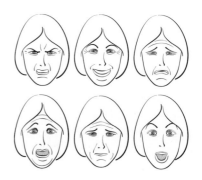

Human safari

This exercise improves your Emotional Intelligence performance by training you to observe others around you and assess their positive EI, displayed verbally and as successful body language. The raw material for this challenge is all around you, in the form of friends and colleagues.

At your next business meeting or social gathering, observe those who seem to be the most effective in the group, and note their successful EI strategies:

- Head held high to show inner confidence

- Verbal acknowledgment of the feelings of other people

- Arms and hands open to show receptivity to the viewpoints of other people

- Body leaning toward the center of the group

- Low, calm tone of voice, revealing well-managed emotions

- Relaxed body posture when handling conflict in others

Movie maker's challenge

Movie makers have become great experts at manipulating an audience's emotions to produce surges of elation or tears of sadness. This exercise teaches you how to recognize the effects others have on you by studying the director's "tricks."

Watch a classic movie. From beginning to end, concentrate on the devices that play on your heartstrings. Try to spot:

- Mood music

- Soft or harsh lighting

- Quick cuts and slow fades

- "Point of view shots" that make you identify more closely with a character

- Character action v. dialogue

- References to people and places that have meaning to everyone, such as mother, home, or friendship

Peacemaker challenge

Reaching a satisfactory conclusion to an argument is one of the highest functions of EI. This exercise teaches you how to negotiate. The best way to learn to manage your own arguments more successfully is by settling other people's. During the coming week, when you come across a colleague, friend, or family member who's engaged in a disagreement, offer to help them work it out.

Follow this pattern for the best peacemaker results:

- Be aware of, and recognize, the emotions of both parties.

- Understand the motivation of both parties.

- Identify any hidden feelings that may not relate immediately to the topic of the argument, like past issues.

- Treat the needs of both parties equally.

- Create an acceptable compromise.

- Express a solution without losing the goodwill of either side.

Judging when to practice this exercise is a useful EI test in itself.

Language and Communication

Language ability status test

This test is similar to those used in hospitals or clinics to assess cognitive ability in relation to language. You can use it to get a picture of whether your language abilities are in top shape. The assessments are on page 182.

- You'll need a friend to administer the test, because the questions either need to be read out loud to you or depend on using material that you haven't already read.
- Don't read the test items yourself, unless you are going to test a friend.
- To perform the tests again, simply replace the given phrases, sentences, or categories with similar ones selected at random from a newspaper.
- You'll need a pencil and paper.

1 *Repetition*
Instructions: Have the subject repeat the following sentence back to you word for word. They should try again if they make a mistake at any point.
Test item: "When Mary preaches to you, she sometimes squeaks like a timid mouse."
Scoring: Perfect, 3 points
1 or 2 mistakes, gets it right second time: 2 points
3 mistakes, stumbles second time: 1 point

2 *Writing*
Instructions: Have the subject write down, word for word, the following sentence.
Test item: "After the first Gulf War, the region enjoyed a period of relative political stability."

Scoring: Perfect, 3 points

1 mistake: 2 points
2 or 3 mistakes, 1 point

3 *Copying*
Instructions: Have the subject read the following sentence one time and then write it down without looking at it again.
Test item: "The ability to acquire language is closely related to the age of the child."

Scoring: Perfect, 3 points
1 mistake: 2 points
2 or 3 mistakes: 1 point

4 *Listing*
Instructions: Have the subject list as many members of a category as possible in one minute. The other person will have to count them (excluding repetitions).

Test item: Any common category will do—e.g., sports, colors, birds, etc.

Scoring: 21 or more: 4 points
17–20: 3 points
13–16: 2 points
12 or less, 1 point

Spelling test

Give the correct spellings of the following words (some are already spelled correctly):

1 uneccesary
2 asassin
3 goverment
4 rythym
5 defendent
6 imminent
7 erorr
8 ambasador
9 indiference
10 alionation
11 reciet
12 assessment
13 parliment
14 independant
15 yoht
16 sedimentery
17 elimenate
18 indefinable
19 doctrinare
20 deferance
21 fuschia
22 minuscule
23 tortoishell
24 puerile

Brainteaser

Dictionary demon

Give yourself and a friend a verbal workout with this popular parlor game. To select a letter to begin with, run your finger over our random letter grid (below) with your eyes shut until your friend says "Stop." You both have two minutes to come up with a word beginning with that letter for each of the following categories:

- Land animal
- Aquatic animal
- Flying animal
- Plant
- Boy's name
- Girl's name
- Country
- Movie star
- City
- Vehicle
- Food
- Brand name
- Famous landmark
- Sport
- Instrument

Q A W S E D X Z
C F R T G V B
H Y U J N M K I
O L P

Score a point for each category that you fill, unless you both pick the same word. To extend the game, choose your own categories.

Body language challenge: dialogue

You can use your knowledge of nonverbal communication to exert more control over conversations and other verbal interactions. The back and forth of conversation is regulated by subtle cues that help with the smooth transition from one person speaking to the other person speaking. Start by observing the cues shown here indicating a desire to interrupt, then progress to using them.

• Slightly raised voice

• Looking away from speaker

• Body movements that match speaker's rhythm but not actual movements

• Triple head nods accompanying verbal cues such as "yes," "well," and so on

• Leaning forward

• Upward hand/arm gestures

• Look for natural dovetailing points (cues that show speaker is winding up)—ends of sentences, drawled final syllables, steady gaze at listener

Body language challenge: persuasion

Improve your grasp of body language by observing its use in daily life. For this challenge, watch politicians on TV and look out for telltale elements of the body language repertoire (check the images on pages 30–33). Notice whether the use of cues correlates to gender or party affiliation.

• **Forward lean:** When is this used, and what does it signal?

• **Eye contact:** How much do they use when talking to interviewers, in comparison with eye contact between normal speakers?

How does this relate to conversational control?

• **Conversational order:** Who has the last word? What is the significance of having or not having the last word?

• **Gestures:** Are they exaggerated? Consider their timing.

• **Handshakes:** What form does a typical politician's handshake take? What does he or she do with the other hand?

• **Nodding and head cocking:** Look at who does these, and how much.

Body language challenge: productivity

People in occupations involving personal contact are more successful if they apply their knowledge of body language. A useful exercise is to watch them doing this. Next time you are in line at an airport check-in counter, waiting to get served at a bar, or some similar situation, see if you can observe staff using anticipatory scanning (looking at people further down the line to anticipate any problems).

• Look to see which staff members steal glances at people yet to be served/farther down the line.

• Look for staff who keep their heads down and don't make eye contact with the customer being served, or who glance at other customers.

• Watch how staff who do scan in anticipatory fashion manage multiple tasks at once.

• Watch to see how successfully these staff deal with customers, and how well customers respond to them.

Secret signals exercise

This game hones your ability to send, receive, and intercept nonverbal messages. You need ideally at least six people sitting in a circle. One is chosen as the "piggy in the middle" (but remains seated) and gives out numbered pieces of paper at random to the seated players. "Piggy" calls two numbers. Those two people must arrange to swap chairs without "piggy" getting to one of their seats first—all without saying a word. If one person loses a seat, he or she becomes "piggy," and the game starts over.

The "piggy" should look out for:

• Hand gestures

• Raised eyebrows

• Head nods

• Very subtle hand/foot gestures

• Eye contact

• Preparatory movements

• Leaning forward/taking weight on feet

• Hands on chair either side of thighs

Word scoring

Develop your verbal, mathematical, and working memory skills with a twist on a popular word game. Here, the aim is to make words out of letters with certain values, and then to add up the values. In this challenge, you begin with a value, and work backward to arrive at the words and letters.

Start by assigning values to all the letters in the alphabet. You can either simply number them 1 through 26, or use the letter–number system described on the Remembering Numbers card. Now use these values to think of words whose letters add up to a set value. Try 50 to begin with. See how many you can get in two minutes. Next time, try a different number.

Upside-down reading

Develop your verbal and spatial abilities by simply turning a newspaper, magazine, or book upside down and reading it from the bottom up. Not only does this require some visual dexterity as you try to work out which letter is which, but it also interrupts your normal smooth perception of grammatical structure, making you work harder to understand sentence structure.

Try reading this upside down from the bottom up:

One of the hallmarks of human intelligence is that it creates its own cultural and social context. It does this through communication, and in particular through the use of language. Language is one of the most complex and advanced cognitive abilities, and yet children far too young to use the bathroom or tie their own shoes seem to master it without effort.

Understanding IQ

Sample IQ test

This test consists of 20 questions of the type and range you might find in an IQ test. There are questions to test your verbal, numerical, spatial, and logical aptitude—some test more than one of these at the same time. To take the test you will need a pen or pencil to record your answers, but do not use a calculator. Allot yourself 45 minutes to complete all the questions. If you can't do a question, move on, but come back to it later. The answers are given on page 182. After you have completed the test, practice the examples for any questions that you have found challenging, then retake the test to monitor your progress.

1   DARK PILE is an anagram of which two four-letter words that mean similar things?

2   What is twice three times forty-five over six?

3   In the diagram below, the color of the shape reflects something about the shape.

Which of the following shapes follows the scheme?

4   Which word can come after all of the following to create five well-known terms?
MONEY   GREEN   ASTEROID
    FAN   BIBLE

5   Pete has two bank accounts: his checking account and his savings account. He transfers $100 from his checking account to his savings account. He now has three times as much money in his savings account as in his checking account and a total of $2,000 in both accounts. What were the balances before the transaction?

6   Arrange the following words in alphabetical order:
SEDUCTION   SEDIMENTATION
SEDULOUS   SEDITIOUS
SEDENTARY   SEDIMENTARY
SEDATIVE   SEDUCTIVE

7   SOLITUDE is to SECLUSION as DEMISE is to _____?

CESSATION CONTINUAL DISTURB VITALITY

8   What comes next in the following sequence: 1, 2, $\frac{2}{3}$, $\frac{8}{3}$, $\frac{8}{15}$, $\frac{16}{15}$, ?

9   Sam has a tile game where any adjacent tile can be moved up or down or sideways into the empty space. It currently looks like this:

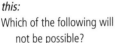

Which of the following will not be possible?

10 Michelle has lost the buttons for the operator keys on her calculator (+, −, x, ÷, though not necessarily in that order). She labels the gaps (A), (B), (C), and (D) and tries some calculations. She learns that:
4 (A) 3 gives the same as 6 (B) 6
4 (C) 6 is less than 8 (D) 3
2 (C) 2 is 4
2 (D) 2 is also 4
Which button is which?

11 Get from the word at the top of the table to the one at the bottom by changing one letter at a time, making a real word at each step.
STEEL

_____

_____

_____

_____

_____

BLIND

12 Which of these shapes is the odd one out?

13 BY IT AIL is an anagram of which seven-letter word?

14 Terri has found the same car on offer at two showrooms, but the owners are asking different prices. She offers them both $2,000 for the car. The first showroom says they'll accept halfway between her offer and their original asking price. The second says they'll knock 20% off the original asking price and then knock off a further $100. If the total of the two original asking prices was $7,500 and the total of the two final offers is $5,700, who should she buy the car from (assuming everything else about the two cars is equal)?

15 Look at the sequence of movements of the man:

Which of the following poses will he be in next?

16 A homophone is a word that sounds the same as another but means something different or is spelled differently. For the following word pair, find the two homophones with the given meanings.

TUBER/PATH

17 Dave and Ingrid have a CD album that has 15 tracks. Dave's preferred playlist starts at track 4 and increases by three tracks each time, giving a playlist of four tracks. Ingrid starts at a track near the end of the album and goes back four tracks each time, also resulting in her listening to four tracks. If Ingrid's playlist has a total (adding the track numbers) of six less than Dave's total, and Ingrid's and David's added together total 62, which track do they both like?

18 Study the following sequence:
[insert images from Sample IQ Test sheet]

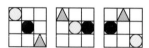

Which of the following shapes comes next:

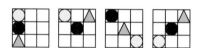

19 Find the hidden 12-letter word by guessing the starting letter and moving between adjacent letters in a horizontal or vertical direction only—diagonal moves are not allowed. Use each letter only once. Guess any missing letters yourself.

E	H	E	
E	C	G	H
S		B	U

20 Which of these isn't from the same cube?

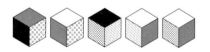

Practice questions

Two-letter words
Timing: 5 minutes each. Difficulty: Tricky. Answers on page 183

Express answers to the following one-word clues using just two letters of the alphabet.

Example: SLIPPERY = IC (ICY)

WIGWAM	CAUTIOUS
BEER	EFFORTLESS
CULTURAL	OVERABUNDANCE

DETERIORATE	JEALOUSY
COLLABORATOR	ATTEMPT
INTERVAL	SUCCEED
BULLETS	RUNDOWN
SECURE	CONSEQUENCES
CLIMBER (PLANT)	PRISON
JUDGE	CROOKED

Alphabetize

Timing: 3 minutes each. Difficulty: Easy.
Answers on page 183

a) *Arrange the following words in alphabetical order:*

MACROCEPHALIC MACRAME

MACKEREL   MACINTOSH

MACHINATE   MACROCOSM

MACHIOLATE   MACROBIOTIC

b) *Arrange the following words in alphabetical order:*

CLATHRATE   CLASSICIST

CLASSICISM   CLASSIFIED

CLASSICAL   CLASSLESS

CLAUDIFICATION CLAUSE

c) *Arrange the following words in alphabetical order:*

DELIMIT   DELINQUENCY

DELINQUENT   DELIGHTFUL

DELIQUESCENCE DELIGHTED

DELINEATE   DELIQUESCE

d) *Arrange the following words in reverse alphabetical order:*

WHOLESOME   WHITTLINGS

WITHERED   WHODUNIT

WHITTLE   WHOEVER

WHOLEHEARTED   WHITHER

e) *Arrange the following words in alphabetical order:*

ECLAMPSIA   ECOCIDE

ECLOGUE   ECHOLOCATE

ECLECTIC   ECLIPSING

ECOLOGY   ECLIPSE

Wordshare

Timing: 5 minutes each. Difficulty: Medium.
Answers on page 184

a) *What property do the following words share?*

TRUST APPLY SHAPE

PLACE FIRE

b) *What property do the following words share?*

SHEAR RING HEARD NEW

FLOUR CREAK ALOUD

c) *What property do the following six-letter words share?*

EFFORT ABHORS BIOPSY

ALMOST BILLOW CHINTZ

ACCESS BIJOUX

d) *What property do the following nouns share?*

WATCH STADIUM OCTOPUS

FISH ARMY

e) What property do the following single-syllable boys' names share?

JACK PETE BILL MARK

PAUL MATT DREW PHIL

f) What property do the following words share?

PRIDE POD TROOP

LITTER FLIGHT

Synonyms
Timing: 25 minutes in total. Difficulty: Tricky.
Answers on page 184

a) EXUBERANCE is to ANGUISH as ACCLAIM is to _____?

RETIREMENT   RENOWN

OBSCURITY   CELEBRITY

b) INCONSEQUENTIAL is to MEAGER as OBLIGATION is to _____?

DEMAND   DEBT

AFFLUENCE   NEED

c) BLOOMING is to VERDANT as NEGLIGENT is to _____?

DISINTERESTED   JUVENILE

DEPENDABLE   DELINQUENT

d) IMPASSIVE is to ANIMATED as AFFABLE is to _____?

CORDIAL   DYSPEPTIC

CONGENIAL   SANGUINE

e) ASSOCIATE is to SEPARATE as BLEAK is to _____?

BARREN   WINDSWEPT

AUSTERE   LUSH

f) CADAVEROUS is to EMACIATED as RANGY is to _____?

SQUAT   MINUSCULE

MAJESTIC   THIN

g) PRACTICAL is to APPLIED as THEORY is to _____?

ASSUMPTION   SUGGESTION

HYPOTHESIS   NOTION

h) ALARM is to COMFORT as ASSUME is to _____?

EXPECT   CONJECTURE

DOUBT   PRESUME

i) JUDGE is to APPRAISE as MASTER is to _____?

CONQUER   PROFICIENT

FAIL   COMPLETE

j) VOLATILE is to STEADY as FEVERISH is to _____?

FEBRILE   TORRID

SULTRY   GELID

Synonyms 2

Timing: 10 minutes in total. Difficulty: Tricky.
Answers on page 184

a) Which two of the following words are
the most similar in meaning?

NUMINOUS   SUNSET

ELEVATED   AURORAL

UNSPEAKABLE   INEFFABLE

b) Which two of the following words are the
most similar in meaning?

INELUCTABLE   EXORBITANT

INDESCRIBABLE GRATUITOUS

UNNECESSARY   CRAFTY

c) Which two of the following words are the
most similar in meaning?

ABSTRACT   DISTANT

REMOVED   ADJACENT

WORTHY   FAMILIAR

Antonyms

Timing: 10 minutes in total. Difficulty: Tricky.
Answers on page 184

a) Which two of the following words are the
most opposite in meaning?

PLEASURE   DELIGHT

UNATTAINABLE   EXQUISITE

CHOICE   CONVENIENT

b) Which two of the following words are the
most opposite in meaning?

SOLAR   NADIR   SUBTERRANEAN

ZENITH   CHTHONIC   APOGEE

c) Which two of the following words are the
most opposite in meaning?

FLOWER   PINE   WOOD

HERBACEOUS   DISDAIN   COPSE

Anagrams

Timing: 25 minutes in total. Difficulty: Medium.
Answers on page 184

a) RANCID HEN is an anagram of which
nine-letter word?

....

b) ME NOOSE is an anagram of which
seven-letter word?

....

c) AUDIT PET is an anagram of which eight-
letter word?

....

d) TRY MI ODOR is an anagram of which
nine-letter word?

....

e) NO LATCH NAN is an anagram of which
ten-letter word?

f) DOE ROCK is an anagram of which
seven-letter word?

....

g) *LEATHER PENS is an anagram of which two organs in the body (6, 5)?*

....

h) *A LAST ALE is an anagram of which three-word phrase (3, 2, 3)?*

....

i) *NO COPY CURT PORK is an anagram of which three types of music?*

....

j) *TACKLE FATE is an anagram of which two words (6, 4) that are opposite in meaning?*

....

k) *A CORDED GEM is an anagram of which two five-letter words of similar meaning?*

....

l) *SUET PIT is an anagram of which three-word phrase (3, 2, 2)?*

....

Missing Words

Timing: 10 minutes each. Answers on page 184

Use the words from the lists following each passage to fill in the blanks in the text.

Difficulty: Medium.

To enter the _____ one had to first find the bogus funeral _____ and then _____ and press the _____ buzzer that was _____ behind the _____ of lilies in the ornate _____. A _____ in a suit would pull back the _____ panel and check you out, and if you successfully _____ this encounter he would _____ the _____ and the whole _____, _____, and all, would _____ back to reveal a flight of stairs.

mechanism	parlor	negotiated	locate	spray
coffin	swing	hidden	secreted	vase
gorilla	sliding	activate	speakeasy	bier

Difficulty: Tricky.

The key to my _____ philosophy, explained the _____, is to _____ the _____ of the _____ with the _____ of the _____, providing all the _____ the former needs to pass the exams while at the same time _____ his or her interest in the _____. The course begins by _____ the _____ aspects of _____ and the first term gives _____ a thorough _____ in the basics.

information	lecturer	needs	educational	covering
essential	grounding	sociology	students	student
rationalize	demands	stimulating	examiners	topic

Letter change
Timing: 15 minutes each. Difficulty: Tricky.
Answers on page 185

Get from the word at the top of the following table to the one at the bottom by changing one letter at a time, making a real word at each step.

ALERT

_____
_____
_____
_____

OMENS

HEART

_____
_____
_____
_____

STONE

LOINS

_____
_____
_____
_____

HONEY

THINK

_____
_____
_____
_____

TRACE

Letter change 2
Timing: 15 minutes. Difficulty: Tricky.
Answers on page 185

Replace the second letter in each word to the left and right of the central blank with the same letter, to give two new English words. Write the letter in the central space. When you've finished, the letters should spell out a six-letter word.

ODES _____ BLEW
SHAM _____ PARK
OVEN _____ AXED
BOAR _____ FULL
WIND _____ TOME
FEAT _____ ABLY

Before and after
Timing: 40 minutes. Difficulty: Tricky.
Answers on page 185

For each word pair, find a word that can come after the word on the left and before the word on the right to make new words or well-known terms.

a) police .... eater

b) clock .... sheet

c) tin .... wrap

d) acid .... dance

e) tea .... board

f) trading .... manager

g) bull .... worm

h) tail .... drift

i) clothes .... power

j) grandfather .... watcher

k) bird .... juice

l) secret .... orange

m) code .... play

n) hard .... candy

o) high .... room

p) comic .... tease

q) brave .... disease

r) well .... time

s) bicycle .... board

t) bag .... line

Investment strategies

Difficulty: Medium. Timing: 5 minutes.
Answer on page 185

A father gives his two sons $1,000 each to invest. Jim loses 30% in the first year, but makes back 50% on the remaining money in the second year. Steve makes 5% in the first year, and another 5% on this in the next. Who has the most to show their father after two years?

Bath night

Difficulty: Easy. Timing: 5 minutes.
Answer on page 185

Samantha uses equal volumes of shampoo, conditioner, and bubble bath each time she has a bath, but they come in different-size bottles. If she currently has the following amounts of each, in which order will she need to replace them?

PRODUCT	Bottle size	Amount remaining
SHAMPOO	250ML	50%
CONDITIONER	300ML	40%
BUBBLE BATH	500ML	26%

Let them eat cake

Difficulty: Tricky. Timing: 10 minutes.
Answer on page 185

Bert the baker makes some pretty disgusting cakes and has a limited supply of eggs, flour, and milk. His recipes use the following quantities (he has other ingredients in vast supply, so don't worry):

RECIPE	Eggs	Flour	Milk
SPONGE CAKE	2	30 OUNCES	1 CUP
CHIFFON CAKE	3	10 OUNCES	2 CUPS
ANGEL FOOD CAKE	1	30 OUNCES	3 CUPS

If Bert has 20 eggs, 200 ounces of flour and 20 cups of milk, what is the maximum number of cakes he can make?

Matter of factorial

Difficulty: Tricky. Timing: 10 minutes.
Answers on page 185

The function "!" is the factorial function (sometimes called "Bang") which means the number multiplied by all of the whole numbers up to it. For example, $5! = 5 \times 4 \times 3 \times 2 \times 1$. Similarly, $3! = 3 \times 2 \times 1$. Therefore, $5!/3! = (5 \times 4 \times 3 \times 2 \times 1) \div (3 \times 2 \times 1)$. You don't have to multiply all these out or even write them all down, as the $3 \times 2 \times 1$ in both parts cancel each other out. You just write down what you are left with, in this case 5×4, which means the answer is 20. Use this technique to simplify the fractions below:

a) $10!/(2!8!)$ ....

b) $(50! \ 29!)/(49!30!)$ ....

c) $(5!8!18!)/(16!6!7!)$ ....

Mirror mirror
Difficulty: Medium. Timing: 10 minutes.
Answer on page 185

Mandy is walking past an antique shop and sees a mirror for sale. She offers the shopkeeper a sum of money, which he says is $10 less than the asking price so he won't accept. The next week the mirror is still there and has been reduced to half price, which is now only $3 more than Mandy originally wanted to pay, so she decides to buy. What does Mandy pay for the mirror?

Bad start to the day
Difficulty: Medium. Timing: 5 minutes.
Answer on page 185

Jan walks to the train station in the mornings. Last Monday she was halfway to her stop when she realized she'd forgotten her keys and had to go back to get them. The second time she left, she got 100 yards down the road before she remembered she'd left the iron on and went back to turn it off. The third time she left, she jumped in a taxi for the last third of the journey as she was running late. If the total distance she walked before reaching the station was 1,800 yards, how far is her house from the station?

Shapes
Difficulty: Medium. Timing: 5 minutes.
Answer on page 185

The numbers given below are the products of (i.e., the results of multiplying) the values of the shapes in the respective row or column. What are the values for each shape?

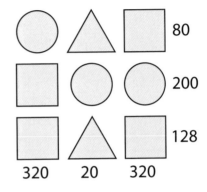

Mmmm, pie
Difficulty: Medium. Timing: 5 minutes.
Answers on page 185

Jeff has to cut up a circular pie for his guests, but the cake is quite tricky to cut and so he wants to use the minimum number of cuts. He is not concerned about the size of the pieces as his guests have different appetites. Assuming that the cake is handed out only after all the cuts have been done, what is the minimum number of cuts needed if he has:

> *a) 4 guests*
>
> *b) 6 guests*
>
> *c) 20 guests*

Hex

Difficulty: Medium. Timing: 5 minutes each.
Answers on page 186

a) *Fill in the gaps in the hexagons, given that each hexagon influences the touching hexagons to their right, but not those above or below.*

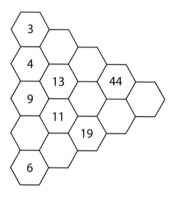

b) *Fill in the gaps in the hexagons, given that each hexagon influences the touching hexagons to their right, but not those above or below. Note that the different types of shading mean the hexagon has a different type of influence.*

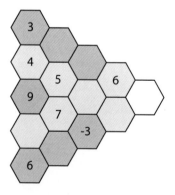

Shopping trip

Difficulty: Medium. Timing: 5 minutes.
Answer on page 186

At her local store Janice is taking advantage of the following special offers:

T-shirts $5 each, three for the price of two

Skirts $7 each, buy one get one free

Sweaters were $10, now 10% off

Janice spends $35 dollars and gets seven items, using a combination of the above offers. (She always gets the extra item on offer.) What did she buy?

Diamonds are forever

Difficulty: Tricky. Timing: 10 minutes.
Answer on page 186

Fill in the values of the remaining spaces (triangles and squares) in the diamond, given that:

- you can use only the numbers 2 to 8 in each remaining triangle, and only once each

- each pair of triangles with adjacent sides has the same total

- the value in a square is the sum of the two triangles adjacent to it

- each pair of diagonally opposite squares (shaded the same) has the same total

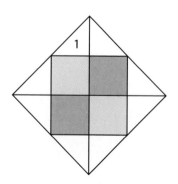

Code words
Difficulty: Medium. Timing: 10 minutes. Answers on page 186

a) *Each of the following letters is worth a different number. The value for the code word is the product of (result of multiplying) the values of the letters. What is the value of the final code word?*

ANNA = 9

NAN = 3

BAN = 6

BANANA = ???

b) *Each of the following letters is worth either 1, 2, 3, or 4 points, but no two letters have the same value. The number given for each word is the total value for that word (with the values of the letters added together). Guess the value of the final code word.*

EGGS: 12

GEESE: 13

SEED: 9

EDGES: ???

Magic squares
Difficulty: Easy. Timing: 5 minutes.
Answer on page 186

a) *Fill in the gaps in the magic square so that no number is repeated and each row, column, and diagonal totals 15.*

	1	
3		
	9	

Difficulty: Medium. Timing: 10 minutes. Answer on page 186

b) *Fill in the gaps in the magic square so that no number is repeated and each row, column, and diagonal totals 34.*

]

		15	4
3		10	
14			1
	11		

Difficulty: Easy.
Timing: 15 minutes.
Answer on page 186

c) Fill in the gaps in the magic square so that no number is repeated within each 3 x 3 box and each row, column, and 3 x 3 box contains all the numbers from 1 to 9.

1			5	6	8			
9	6			7			3	
7						6	2	
		8	1		2	5		
5	9	3		4		7	1	2
		6	7		9	8		
	4	9						1
	2			1			5	6
			9	2	7			4

Difficulty: Medium.
Timing: 15 minutes.
Answer on page 186

d) Fill in the gaps in the magic square so that no number is repeated within each 3 x 3 box and each row, column, and 3 x 3 box contains all the numbers from 1 to 9.

		9				2		4
1		7				6		
3			8	9	4			5
						9		3
7			4		2			1
4		5						
9			5	6	7			2
		3				5		9
5		8				4		

Difficulty: Medium.
Timing: 25 minutes.
Answer on page 187

e) Fill in the gaps in the magic square so that no number is repeated within each 3 x 3 box and each row, column, and 3 x 3 box contains all the numbers from 1 to 9.

2			4	9	7			5
	1						9	
						4	2	8
		2				3		
8		7	6		1	5		9
		5				6		
4	6	3						
	2						7	
9			5	8	3			4

Difficulty: Tricky.
Timing: 35 minutes.
Answer on page 187

f) Fill in the gaps in the magic square so that no number is repeated within each 3 x 3 box and each row, column, and 3 x 3 box contains all the numbers from 1 to 9.

	5	2						
6						7	3	
			9	1	4			
	2	8						7
			3	6	5			
9						1	4	
			7	2	8			
	3	1						9
						8	6	

How You Remember

Memory and Concentration

General knowledge quiz

General knowledge is a form of long-term semantic memory. This quiz tests your general knowledge by asking you to recall facts you would have learned at school, and have probably encountered since.

Write your answers on a separate sheet of paper. The answers are on pages 187.

1 Name the nine planets of the solar system.

2 Name the start and end dates (month and year only) for World War I and World War II (giving the months of both VE and VJ Days for the latter).

3 Name all the continents and oceans.

4 Name three tragedies, three comedies, and three history plays, all by Shakespeare.

5 Name the capitals of the following countries:

Norway	Sweden
Switzerland	Canada
Chile	Peru
South Africa	Egypt
Kenya	Australia
Malaysia	Pakistan
Iran	Ukraine.

6 Name the four longest rivers in the world.

7 "I wandered lonely as a cloud... "— Give the next three lines.

8 Complete the mathematical formula: The square of the hypotenuse = ?

9 What are the names of the following two physical laws?
a) For a fixed mass of gas at constant temperature, the pressure and volume are inversely proportional, i.e., pV = constant.

b) When applied to springs, a small extension, x, of the spring exerts a proportional restoring force, $F = -kx$, where k is a constant, a measure of the spring's stiffness.

Short-term memory quiz

Short-term memory loss can cause great frustration through trivial but irritating failures. Use this test to assess the current state of your STM, and return to check your progress. The answers are on page 188.

1   *Can you recall the exact locations of the following items in and around your house?*
a) The keys to your front door

....

b) The keys to your car

....

c) The keys to your back door and windows

....

(1 point for each)

2   *Write down what you had to eat...*
a) For your last meal:

....

(1 point)

b) For the meal before that:

....

(1 point)

c) For the meal before that:

....

(2 points)

3   *Aside from anyone who lives at home with you, can you recall the identity of the first person you met today (whom you know)?*

....

(if yes, score 1)

4   *Write down the names and numbers of the last five people you have telephoned.*
Name   Number

a) ....

(1 point if both)

b) ....

(1 point for each)

c) ....

(1 point for name, 2 for number)

d) ....

(1 point for name, 2 for number)

e) ....

(1 point for name, 3 for number)

5   *Write down the names of the last five people who called you, and what they wanted to talk about*

a) ....

(1 point if both)

b) ....

(1 point for each)

c) ....

(1 point for name, 2 for topic)

d) ....

(1 point for name, 2 for topic)

e) ....

(1 point for name, 3 for topic)

6   *Can you recall the last commercial that you saw on TV, including the product that was being advertised and the theme of the commercial?*

....

....

(1 point for theme, 3 for product)

Brainstormers

Digit-span test

Your digit-span—the number of digits you can accurately recall—is a measure of the power of your memory. Read each of the following series aloud, slowly, then write it down. How far through the list can you get?

8461

62964

167490

9056407

32091654

580163928

0366192745

49012640926

58016392846173

32941937602291

33162964810986

45372817274325

98970366192745

The average digit-span is seven digits. Whether yours is better or worse than the average, you can learn simple tricks to transform your ability to remember things like telephone numbers.

Decay

In the previous exercise you tested your short-term memory to see how many digits in a row you could recall. To see for yourself how quickly this type of memory "decays," try the following:

1   *Learn one of the 14-digit lists above and take the digit-span test, then record the number of digits you recalled as your score.*

2   *Do something else for one minute, then try to remember the list again, and record your score.*

3   *After another minute or two, repeat the process.*

Record your score here: ....

Score after 1 minute: ....

Score after 2–3 minutes: ....

Letter-span test

Your working memory has a limited capacity, but it doesn't only store numbers. In fact, it stores phonemes—units of auditory/verbal information, which can mean numbers, or simply syllables or letters. Give your working memory an alternative workout by practicing and trying to enlarge your letter-span using the letters below.

With each of the following series of letters, read the series aloud, slowly, then cover the page and write down the series on a piece of paper. How far down the list can you get before you start forgetting letters?

GYTC

FPLDW

EGHJDZ

VCHASPQ

JOPEWITVB

MDKFRZPMSA

IWGPUTUEXJK

FLLIYABGRTMQ

CXFVOTKFARBZD

The average letter span is 7 digits.

Memory-house challenge

Printed below is a floorplan of a house, with 10 locations: bedroom, bathroom, study, top of the stairs, stairs, entry hall, kitchen, garden, dining room, and cupboard.

Below are three lists of items for you to memorize:

Office supplies list
Writing paper
Stapler
Hole-punch
Red pen
Blue pen
Pen mug
Memo forms
Address book
Internal phonebook
Printer cartridge

Fantasy shopping list
Scented candles
Cashmere socks
Bath salts
Bestselling book
Box of Belgian chocolates
DVD of Italian opera
Embroidered pillow
Diamanté bracelet
Sterling silver money clip
Vintage wine

Vacation packing list
4 towels
Tanning lotion
Silk dress
Lightweight suit
Thong sandals (2 pairs)
Bikini
Swim shorts
Jogging suit
Waterproof watches
Diving certificates

Photocopy the floorplan three times. Using the office supplies list, write one item in each of the suitable locations. Memorize the items by associating each with the location you have placed it in. Cover the page. When you come to recall the information, mentally journey through the house, recalling each chunk as you go. See how many items you can remember 15, 45 minutes and 2 hours later. Record your scores (one point for each item) overleaf.

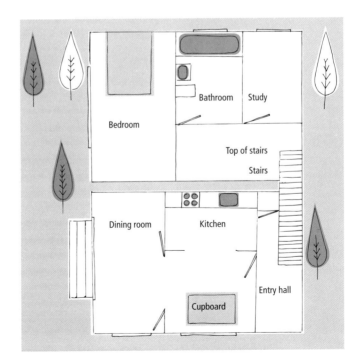

Office supplies list

Score after 15 minutes:

....

Score after 45 minutes:

....

Score after 2 hours:

....

On fresh photocopies, repeat the process using the fantasy shopping list and the vacation packing list. Record your scores below to check your progress.

Fantasy shopping list

Score after 15 minutes:

....

Score after 45 minutes:

....

Score after 2 hours:

....

Vacation packing list

Score after 15 minutes:

....

Score after 45 minutes:

....

Score after 2 hours:

....

Changed order

Classroom reunited

Testing the limits of your memory can help to extend those limits. Develop your memory for the distant past by trying this challenge. You'll need a pen or pencil and paper.

Think back to your school days, and write down the names of as many of your classmates and teachers as you can manage. Next to each name, write the most detailed description of appearance, habits, and background that you can remember. Return to your list over succeeding days. You may be surprised at how much comes back to you when you start exploring your memory.

Alternative versions

Memory is partly a constructive process, which means that when you remember something, you actually construct your memory anew. This is especially true of episodic memory—memory for events and situations, for things that happened to you. This can make for an amusing game.

- Gather together a group of friends who were all previously present at the same event—such as a party, graduation ceremony, or wedding.

- Draw up a list of memory categories—e.g. what kind of food was served or who was wearing what.

- Have everyone write down what they recall for each category.

- Go around the group, reading out memories to see whether there is a high level of agreement. You may be surprised at how people's recollections differ, and at how much you'd forgotten but other people remembered.

Kim's game

Test your short-term memory with this classic memory game. Each illustration incudes a host of items. Pick one of the illustrations and give yourself exactly 30 seconds (you'll need a timer) to memorize as many of the items as possible. Turn away to recall the items. When another two minutes have elapsed, write down as many of the items as you can remember then check your results against the illustration. As you improve, increase the number of illustrations you use.

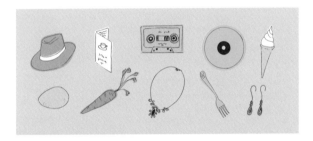

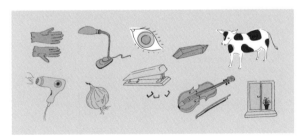

Memory Processing

Brainstormers

Enrich your recall

No matter how mundane you think your day may have been, try to use your experiences to improve general recall and thus the quality of your encoding of things that you want to remember. Think about all these elements of your day:

- The world around you
- Events of the day
- People you met
- The part of the day you most enjoyed
- One surprising event or experience

1   *Try to recall the first view you had of the outside world when you left home this morning. Write down:*

ambient sounds and noises

....

....

....

the smell outside (of traffic, grass, etc.)

....

....

the whole scene around you

....

....

....

2   *Try to recall the key facts you read in a recent newspaper article. Write down:*

the general subject of the article

....

....

....

how the issue related to others in the paper

....

....

....

Now try to recall:

the date of the event

....

any numbers involved (e.g., statistics)

....

....

....

the names of the people involved

....

....

3 Try to remember three people you met for the first time today. Write down:

where you met them

....

what you were doing at the time

....

....

what you first noticed about them

....

....

....

Now try to recall their names:

1: ....

2: ....

3: ....

Recall with acrostics

Devise your own acrostics to help you with the tasks listed below:

- Spell difficult words: e.g., to spell YACHT, use Yelling Across Classrooms Helps Teachers.
- Remember lists: e.g., This Elephant Means Prizes could be an acrostic for a shopping list consisting of Tomatoes, Eggs, Milk, and Pasta.
- Learn important information.

Begin with short lists and move on to something more challenging, like the zodiac constellations. Improve your acrostic-making skills by thinking up acrostics to help you remember the following:

1 How to spell inoculate, innocuous, succulent, truculent

2 The seven deadly sins (pride, covetousness, lust, anger, gluttony, envy, and sloth)

3 The seven continents, in order of size (Asia, Africa, North America, South America, Antarctica, Europe, Australasia)

4 The five biological kingdoms (Monera, Protista, Fungi, Plantae, Animalia)

5 The animal signs of Chinese astrology, in order (the Rat, Ox, Tiger, Rabbit, Dragon, Snake, Horse, Goat, Monkey, Rooster, Dog, Pig)

The PQRST study system

Get the most out of learning, revision, or reading with the PQRST study system.

- P is for Preview. Preview the material you need to learn by skimming through it and looking at the headings and topics so that you know what is covered and what you should expect to learn.
- Q is for Question. Write down questions you should be able to answer.
- R is for Read. Read the material thoroughly with an eye to finding the answers to your questions.
- S is for Summarize. Summarize for yourself what you have just read, reciting or jotting down the main points.
- T is for Test. Later, but within 24 hours, test yourself using the questions you posed.

Use this sample text from a stress-management book to practice the PQRST system:

If you aren't a good planner, look on the bright side and think of all the other things you manage to do because you are not always obsessively making lists of things to do! Creative people in particular seem to thrive in a degree of disorganization. However, most people will find their stress levels are brought down to reasonable levels if they can actually find that important phone number or file.

Actually, many of us have split personalities when it comes to being organized. We might be fiercely effic-ient when at work while our private lives flounder in a mound of clutter and lack of time. In part, this might be a self-defence mechanism. Who wants to be a totally efficient automaton 24 hours a day, 7 days a week? But it can go too far, and home disorganization, which contrasts so much with our professional lives, can end up impacting on professional capabilities and encourage feelings of being out of control.
Prioritizing is another vital skill you should learn. It's astounding how, when there is an important job to do, it suddenly seems so important to make the coffee, call your mother, or walk the dog. If you habitually procrastinate, make a point of making a daily plan.

Preview the material by perusing it briefly.

1   Now write three questions about the piece.

i) ....

ii) ....

iii) ....

2   Read thoroughly and summarize the main points:

i) ....

ii) ....

iii) ....

3   Cover up your answers and don't look at them or the extract again for a day. Now test yourself to see how many of the key points of the piece you can remember.

i) ....

ii) ....

iii) ....

Group memory game
This fun exercise illustrates the way memories are constructed from fragments that your mind "stitches" together into a coherent narrative.

Gather some friends together, and think back to a recent event, such as a party or a wedding, which you all attended. Give each person a photocopied set of the questions below. Allow 10 minutes for the answers, then read out what everyone wrote for each question. You will be surprised to find how differently people remember the same thing.

1   Name the event, time, and date:

....

2   Name as many guests as you can:

....

....

....

3   What food was served?

....

4   What were you offered to drink?

....

....

5 *Whom did you chat to?*

....

....

6 *Where did you sit or stand?*

....

....

7 *Whom were you surprised to see?*

....

....

8 *Who was notable by their absence?*

....

....

9 *Name three songs that were played:*

....

....

....

10 *What time did you leave?*

....

rhymes for them, perhaps based on a personal characteristic or hobbies, as in the examples in the workbook.

• To remember shopping or other lists by thinking up rhymes for items on the list or making up a rhyme out of associated words.

Use the list of names and the personal characteristic that goes with each one, to make an image that helps you remember names and identities. For example, Jeannine—who loves to bake—can be rhymed with whip cream.

1 Neil, vegetarian:

....

2 Jack, poker genius:

....

3 Linda, mother of many:

....

Use rhyme to remember

One of the oldest and simplest mnemonic strategies is the rhyme, because one word or line "cues" the memory of the next. Use rhymes:

• To enhance the power of associations in other mnemonic strategies.

• To remember names by making up silly

Speed-reading for success

When skimming text to extract the maximum information in the minimum time, follow these tips:

- Know what information you want to extract before you start reading.

- Skim irrelevant details and linger on key points.

- Force the pace—move on faster than normal.

- Guide your eye movements with the tip of a pencil or ruler to avoid automatically skipping back to material you've read.

- Review what you've read afterward, at first by making short notes but later purely mentally.

- Test yourself half an hour later to see what you've retained.

- Try the speed-reading exercise in the workbook.

Pick the lead article on page 3 of today's newspaper to practice your speed-reading skills. After you have read the piece, record here three key points:

1: ....

2: ....

3: ....

Take the memory journey

To remember the order of anything that can be divided up into stages or chunks—such as lists or speeches—use a real-life memory journey.

1   Draw a journey you know well.

2   Work out, and sketch or mark in the workbook, a series of easy-to-remember stops on the journey at points such as intersections, particular stores, a mailbox—whatever exists on the actual journey.

3   When committing something to memory, associate each item with a stop on the journey. To make the material even easier to remember, you could turn the journey into a story.

1: ....

2: ....

3: ....

4: ....

5: ....

6: ....

7: ....

Walk down memory lane

Think of a street you know like the back of your hand, such as the street you walk along to get to work or school, and test yourself to see whether you can really remember it.

1   Picture the street in your mind's eye and describe aloud the buildings in sequence along each side, together with any landmarks such as intersections, traffic lights, trees, or mailboxes.

2   Say aloud the names of any shops, businesses, or office blocks.

3   Picture the look and color of house fronts, shop fronts, awnings, etc.

4   Sketch a detailed plan of the street from a bird's eye view, with all these details added.

5   Next time you visit the street mark yourself for accuracy and how many features you recalled.

Memory Problem Solver

Brainstormers

Daily review for recall

To improve episodic or autobiographical memory (for the events of your life), review the past day. At the end of each day, sit on your own somewhere quiet, and mentally review the day. Think about everything that has happened and practice with the following prompts:

- What you did

- Whom you spoke to

- What they said

- Where you were

- What it was like there

- What you achieved

- What was the weather like?

- Whom did you enjoy and whom did you get irritated at?

- What part of the day did you most enjoy?

- Recall three interesting newspaper/Internet articles you saw.

Part-wording booster

Use part-wording to make long, difficult words and complex foreign names much easier to remember.

1   Look at how the word breaks up into chunks, syllables, or similar words—e.g.,

the name Clemenceau (a notable 20th-century French prime minister) suggests the word "clement."

2   Use the part-word to create a memorable association—e.g. "clement" could be used to mean "fine weather" or could be extended to the citrus fruit "clementine."

3   Use the association for a visualization.

The words below have been broken into chunks to make their meanings easier to remember, through the technique of part-wording. Suggestions for visualizations are given, but feel free to think of your own, and write them after the examples.

Syco-phant
(try a psychologist making eyes at an elephant):

....

Nefar-ious
(try a threatening landscape far away):

....

Met-ic-ulous
(try a mat with carefully ticked or checked boxes):

....

Grand-iloquent
(try a floating king):

....

Boost precious memories

If you wish you could remember more about your childhood and family background, try drawing a family tree. Either fill in the names of your immediate forebears in the chart or follow the instructions below.

1   Write your name on a large piece of paper. Around your name, note basic information (e.g., where you were born, the different addresses where you have lived, the names of your schools, what your first job was, where you met your partner).

2   Beneath your name, draw lines and add your parents' names. In a circle around each name, note information you can remember about them.

3   Add the names of any siblings and draw lines between them and your parents. Around each of them, make notes.

4   Repeat the process to include more distant relatives in your family tree.

Circle of friends

Use the spider-diagram method to explore your memory of friends and your wider social circle. As well as being an excellent test of recall, this is a good way to improve your autobiographical memory. Consisting of circles with lines radiating out from them to other circles, spider diagrams can be used to represent how memories are stored in your brain.

1   Write your name in a circle in the middle of a large piece of paper.

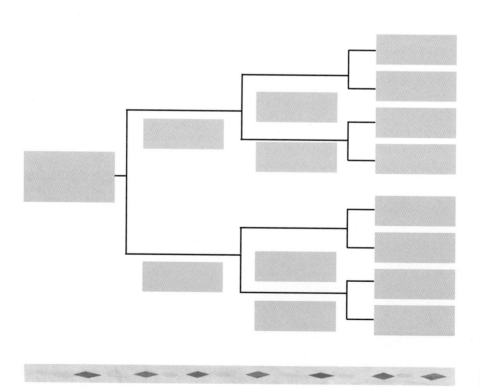

2   *Draw lines from it out to a ring of other circles, as in the workbook, and write your friends' names in those. Add where you met them and how long you've known them.*

3   *Draw more lines and circles for friends of friends. Try to list the same info about them. Continue in this way, seeing how much you can remember about people you've met.*

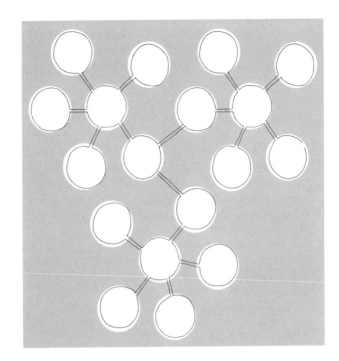

Restyle facts as questions

Here's how to remember those nuggets of information that you know could come in handy one day if only you could remember them. Simply restyle the information, breaking it up into question form as if you were being asked about it in a quiz or a test.

- What is the main point of this material?
- If there is one piece of information that is most important, what is it?
- Which part do I find the most interesting?
- Why is this information interesting in general?

The first paragraph, on the problems of jet lag, is followed by a list of questions, which are examples of how to restyle facts and information to make it more memorable. Try the technique yourself and create a list of questions on the second paragraph, which is about how to beat jet lag.

Paragraph 1

If you travel across time zones, you are likely to be affected by jet lag as your body struggles to adapt to the day/night cycle in your new location. Even experienced air crew suffer from jet lag. Jet lag seems to be worse flying west to east around the globe, rather than the other way round.

1 When are you most likely to get jet lag?

....

....

2 Does regular flying cut down the risk?

....

....

3 On which journeys can jet leg appear worse?

....

Paragraph 2

Try these simple adjustments to help reduce the effects of jet lag. Once you are on the flight, adjust your watch to the time at your destination. Also, if your stay is a short one, say two or three days, keep to your home schedule and make appointments and go to sleep accordingly. Keep hydrated on the flight by drinking lots of water and no alcohol. This will make you less likely to suffer from jet lag. Avoid caffeine, and take an eye mask with you to help you sleep when it is light.

Question 1:

....

Question 2:

....

Question 3:

....

The number–shape system

Turn forgettable numbers into memorable mental pictures by using images suggested by their shapes.

Some classic number–shape associations are:
1—a pencil; 2—a swan; 3—lips;
4—a sail; 5—a seahorse; 6—a bat and ball;
7—a boomerang; 8—an hourglass;
9—a balloon on a string; 0—a ring

The visual associations for each number can be made into stories to help remember short strings of numbers relatively easily. Using the images below, record your visualizations for the following sets of numbers, drawing them in the boxes:

287

3541

62389

The number–letter system

Convert numbers into letters and use these in a mnemonic device, such as the following:

- Initial pairs: use a pair of letters to form the name of a memorable celebrity.

- Mnemonic acronym: use the letters to trigger a memorable sentence.

Use the number–letter pairs below, or devise your own pairs.

Use this number–letter system, or a similar system of your own devising, to make up words or acronyms for the following numbers. The first number has some examples here already.

1 = B	0 = K	9 = T
2 = C	1 = L	0 = U
3 = D	2 = M	1 = V
4 = E	3 = N	2 = W
5 = F	4 = O	3 = X
6 = G	5 = P	4 = Y
7 = H	6 = Q	5 = Z
8 = I	7 = R	
9 = J	8 = S	

9034 (could use JADE, TUNO, JUDY):
....
....
....

3090:
....
....
....

87054:
....
....
....

Remember your PIN

Break a string of four numbers down into chunks and look for memorable internal associations.

- Are successive numbers multiples of one another (e.g. 3924)?

- Is there a progressive sequence in the number (e.g. 2468)?

- Does the first half relate to the second half (e.g. 3723, in which the first half adds up to 10, while the second half adds up to half of that sum)?

Try to find internal associations for the following PINs to make them more memorable, and note down how the digits relate to each other in each set:

6547:
1265:
4836:
2439:

Can you recall all four PINs at once?

....
....

Brain-boosting Strategies

Brainstormers

Use these questions to hone your basic IQ skills—improving your mental speed, your creativity and your critical faculties.

Caesar cipher challenge

Timing: 3 minutes. Difficulty: Easy.
Answer on page 188

Since the earliest known ciphers, which date back to ancient times, code-breaking has been a test of intelligence, in which the code-breaker's cleverness could mean the difference between victory and defeat, life and death. Breaking codes is also a good way to exercise the gray matter and keep your mind honed. This exercise involves one of the simpler types of codes, known as the Caesar Cipher because Julius Caesar employed a version of it during his campaigns in ancient Gaul. In the Caesar Cipher, each letter of the message to be coded (known as the plaintext) is replaced with a letter farther on in the alphabet—this is called a letter shift. For instance, a single-letter shift would mean that every "A" in the plaintext would be replaced with a "B," every "B" with a "C," and so on. A five-letter shift would mean that every "A" would be replaced with an "F," every "B" with a "G," etc. Now that you know how the Caesar Cipher works, try to break the code and decipher this message:

J DBNF, J TBX, J DPORVFSFE

Caesar cipher challenge II

Timing: 30 minutes in total. Difficulty: Tricky.
Answer on page 188

Below is a series of encrypted messages, using shifts of varying degrees. (For example, one might be encoded with a single-letter shift cipher, but the next might involve a four-letter shift.)

a) *BMM UIF LJOH'T NFO*

b) *IPNF TXFFU IPNF*

c) *IPX NBOZ SPBET NVTU B NBO XBML EPXO?*

d) *JG YJQ NCWIJU NCUV, NCWIJU DGUV*

e) *TSHJ ZUTS F YNRJ*

f) *U OMZ'F SQF ZA EMFUERMOFUAZ*

g) *SX DRO LVOKU WSNGSXDOB*

h) *QDGC XC IWT JHP, X LPH QDGC XC IWT JHP*

i) *CXY XO CQN FXAUM, VJ, CXY XO CQN FXAUM*

j) *VNF IJO AJM RCJH OCZ WZGG OJGGN*

Follow the instructions
Timing: 3 minutes each. Difficulty: Easy.
Answer on page 188

a) Look at the letters below. Which letter is the third to the right of the letter second to the left of the letter to the right of the letter after F?

    D E F G H J K L

b) Look at the letters below. Which letter is just to the left of the fifth letter to the right of the third letter after the letter that is 23rd in the alphabet?

    Q W E R T Y U I O P

Rebus
Timing: 5 minutes. Difficulty: Easy.
Answer on page 188

A rebus is a puzzle where syllables or words are represented by pictures. In the rebus shown below, what word does the sequence of pictures spell out?

Rebus II
Timing: 10 minutes. Difficulty: Medium.
Answer on page 188

In the rebus shown below, what phrase does the sequence of pictures spell out?

Rebus III
Timing: 10 minutes. Difficulty: Tricky.
Answer on page 188

In the rebus shown below, what phrase does the sequence of pictures spell out?

Dice game
Difficulty: Tricky. Timing: 10 minutes.
Answer on page 189

Daniel and Pete are having a dice game, where they each bet $2 and then roll a fair, six-sided dice. If one rolls higher than the other, he wins and gets all the money, otherwise they share it. Brandon wants to play, but they don't have another dice, so they say that he can bet $1 and he wins all the money when they tie. Should Brandon accept these rules and play, or is he likely to lose out?

Dinner party
Difficulty: Medium. Timing: 5 minutes.
Answer on page 189

Ron and Janet are having a dinner party where they and two other couples are to be seated around a round table. If they insist that no couples sit next to each other and that sexes must alternate, how many unique arrangements exist? (To qualify as a "unique arrangement," each person must be seated between different people than in other arrangements.)

What about if there are eight people instead of six?

Knight, knight
Difficulty: Medium.
Timing: 5 minutes.
Answer on page 189

In chess, a knight can make the moves shown in the diagram on the right:

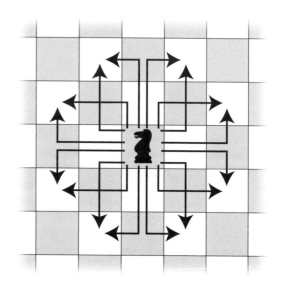

> *What is the minimum number of moves in which a knight can reach all the squares on an 8 by 8 board if it starts in the bottom left corner? (Each of the L-shaped moves shown in the diagram counts as one move.)*

Later, elevator
Difficulty: Tricky. Timing: 5 minutes.
Answer on page 189

Bob got in the elevator but forgot to press the button. He went down 13 floors and somebody got in. They then went to a floor with twice the number of the floor Bob wanted. The other person got out and the elevator went back down four floors, where someone else got in and took it to the floor with three times the number Bob wanted. Bob eventually got a chance to press the button and go to the floor he wanted. Later at his desk he realized he had traveled for 78 floors in total. He needed to travel only four floors, and he ended up at a lower floor to where he started. Where did he start and finish?

The Brain Power Lifestyle

Sleeping and Relaxation

Brainstormers

Top to toe relaxation

Good for your muscles and your mind, this exercise involves trying to relax every muscle in your body:

- *Start off by lying down somewhere quiet, warm, and comfortable.*

- *Close your eyes and tense every muscle in your body as hard as you can manage. Hold them like that for a few seconds and then release.*

- *Now focus on your toes. Try to will them to relax. Concentrate on how they feel; sense them; then feel them relaxing.*

- *Repeat this for every part of your feet, starting with the soles, then moving to your heels, and then to your ankles.*

- *Work your way up your body, repeating the same sequence of concentration, sensation, and relaxation. Do this for every single muscle group, front and back.*

- *When you get to your chest, concentrate on your fingers and work up the arms to your shoulders. Then move up the neck, head, and face, finishing with your scalp.*

Meditation exercise

This meditation exercises your memory and provides a relaxation technique to help de-stress your life.

1 *Pick a quiet, comfortable place where you won't be disturbed, dim the lights, and sit down.*

2 *Picture a scene from your memory, such as your last vacation.*

3 *Now bring your visualization to life by focusing on details as if you were experiencing them.*

4 *Feel the warmth of the sun on your skin. Smell the odors. Picture the brightness and the colors, and hear the sounds.*

5 *Try to recall individuals' faces and conversations.*

Meditation exercise II

This exercise allows you to test your memory and helps you relax. Follow the steps of the previous exercise but instead of steps 2 and 4, picture a scene from your childhood memories, such as a visit to the zoo or your first day at school. Visualize all of the following in detail:

- *The layout of the place and its main landmarks*

- *People who would have been present at the time*

- *What size you were*

- *Whether you were excited, happy, or relaxed*

Meditation exercise III

This meditation exercise will also stretch your memory as well as being an effective relaxation technique. Again, go back to the first exercise but instead of steps 2 and 4, think back to your first kiss.

- *Try to remember the name and appearance of the other person.*

- *Go over the events that led up to the kiss.*

- *Think about the details of the place where it happened.*

- *Try to recall incidental details such as the music that was playing.*

Meditation exercise IV

As well as challenging your memory powers, meditation can also help you de-stress. Follow the steps in the first exercise but instead of steps 2 and 4, picture a significant happy event in your life, such as your graduation, your wedding, or the birth of your first child. Visualize external details such as the following:

- *What you were wearing*

- *What the weather was like*

- *What music was being played*

- *How you felt and whether you had any strange thoughts*

Bust anxiety and breathe

Anxiety interferes with recall, often when you need it to be at its best. Try this relaxation technique to clear anxiety and focus your mind.

1   *Sit back in your chair but don't slump.*

2   *Put one hand on your chest and one on your upper abdomen, so that you can feel them moving up and down as you breathe.*

3   *As you inhale, expand your chest as little as possible; instead, consciously expand your abdomen.*

4   *To start with, you might need to take big breaths—take them slowly (one every 10 seconds, or 6 per minute).*

5   *Work up to taking slightly smaller breaths—about 10–12 per minute.*

Practice this technique enough and you will be able to use it to boost your focus in almost any situation.

Answers

How Are You Wired?
Assess your strengths and weaknesses

Scoring

Q	a	b	c
1	3	1	2
2	1	2	3
3	3	1	2
4	2	3	1
5	3	2	1
6	3	1	2
7	3	2	1
8	1	2	3
9	3	1	2
10	1	2	3
11	1	2	3
12	2	1	3
13	3	2	1
14	2	3	1
15	3	2	1
16	3	2	1
17	2	3	1
18	2	1	3
19	1	2	3
20	3	1	2
21	1	1	3
22	1	3	2
23	1	1	3

How did you score?

23–36: You have a low opinion of your mental abilities and may also be lacking vital knowledge about how to look after your brain and maintain its capacity. Maybe some aspects are letting you down more than others—work on these, and you can boost both your mental powers and your self-esteem.

37–56: You share similar overall levels of ability with the vast majority of your family members, friends, and colleagues, but your individual mental makeup has its own unique pattern, with strengths on which you can build and weaknesses you need to tackle.

57–69: You have a high opinion of your own mental abilities, and are well informed about how to get the most out of your brain.

Intelligence and Forward Thinking
IQ-style test

Score 1 point for each correct answer

1: b; 2: d; 3: b; 4: c; 5: c; 6: a; 7: c; 8: a; 9: d; 10: d; 11: c; 12: d; 13: b;14: b; 15: center, 2nd row; 16: 5..

How did you score?

5 or less: Below average • 6–11: Average • 12–14: Above average • 15–16: Gifted

Break down your score into the three different abilities tested here. Questions 1–7 test your verbal reasoning ability; questions 8–14 test your numerical reasoning ability; questions 15–16 test your spatial reasoning ability. Did you get fewer than half the questions right in any of these categories? If so, this could be an area on which you need to work.

Don't take your result too seriously—this is not a standardized intelligence test and cannot be used to accurately ascertain your IQ. For that, you'll need a full-length IQ test, such as the Stanford–Binet Scale or Wechsler Adult-Intelligence Scale, with dozens of items that need to be done under timed conditions.

Creativity and Lateral Thinking

Score 1 point for each correct answer.

1: The remote associates test
Answers: a: back; b: party; c: book; d: play; e: paper; f: match; g: cheese; h: quick.

2: The fox, corn, and chicken puzzle
Solution: You have to take the chicken across, leave her on the far bank, and then come back and pick up the fox and ferry him across. You are now on the far bank with the fox and the chicken. Next, crucially, you take the chicken back with you to the near bank, swap her for the corn, leave the corn with the fox on the far bank, and come back to pick up the chicken.
Comment To solve this problem, you have to make the conceptual leap to realizing that you can carry items both ways! Because of the way the problem is stated, it doesn't occur to most people that this is possible—it requires either a flash of lateral thinking, or a lot of head-scratching until the answer is stumbled upon by accident.

3: The bus driver riddle
Solution: The bus driver's name is your name! You were told at the start to "imagine that you are a bus driver."
Comment: Most people dismiss this as a dumb joke that cannot be answered because they focus on the wrong information. They assume, while reading the riddle, that it must conform to the usual pattern for numerical/mathemat-

ical riddles (i.e., they assume that you have to do mental arithmetic to keep track of who is on the bus). The nonconformist or creative thinker is able to overcome misleading assumptions like this, and find his or her way to a solution by focusing only on the critical elements of a problem.

4: The nine-dot problem

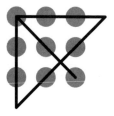

Comment: Many people have trouble with this one because they can't break free of the mind-set that views the nine dots as a square. The concept of a square has functional fixedness, carrying with it the assumption that you can't extend your lines beyond the "boundaries" of the square. Only by breaking free of this mind-set, and literally thinking outside the box, can you find the solution.

5: The messenger's problem
Solution: Use two support trucks in addition to your own. All three of you set off for one day's drive, using up a can of fuel each, at the end of which the first truck transfers one can of fuel to you and one can to the remaining support truck, so that both of you are once again carrying the maximum number of fuel cans. The first truck then has enough fuel to drive one day back to home base. You and the other truck carry on for another day, again using up a can of fuel each. At the end of the day the second truck transfers one can of fuel to you, leaving him with two cans (enough to get back to base) and you with a full load of four

cans—enough to get to the other base and deliver your message.

Comment: The conceptual hurdle that you have to overcome to solve this problem is to realize that the support trucks have to accompany you only part of the way, and don't have to travel the same distance as each other. The creative thinker realizes there is no rule that says all the trucks need to go all the way.

How did you score?

9 or more: You are good at making connections—put your talents to good use by trying the Creativity Exercises.

6–8: You need to loosen up your thinking processes.

Less than 6: You are having trouble making new connections. The Creativity and Lateral Thinking cards can help you get into a more creative mind-set.

Emotional intelligence— EQ-style test

Inventory

Use the following key to work out your score for the Inventory.

Scoring

Q	a	b
1	0	1
2	0	1
3	0	1
4	1	0
5	0	1
6	0	1
7	1	0
8	0	1
9	1	0
10	0	1
11	0	1
12	0	1
13	1	0
14	0	1

Emotional understanding test

1a: anger; b: happiness; c: fear; d: sadness. Score 1 point for each correct answer.
2: a: 1 point, b: 0 points, c: 3 points.

How did you score?

For your EQ score, add your score on the Emotion Understanding Test to your score from the Inventory.

18 and above: You probably have high EI. You are good at understanding your own internal emotional processes and reading how other people feel, and can also use this knowledge to get on well with people and negotiate social situations successfully. A high EQ suggests that you might thrive in a career involving people management or personal contact (e.g., sales, human resources, caring profession, etc.). Don't take your abilities for granted, however—you need to keep them honed.

11–17: Your EI is probably within the average range. You do your best to be sensitive and empathetic, and keep your emotions in check where necessary, but it's not always easy. And while on the whole you try to get on with family, friends, and colleagues, you don't always manage your relationships to best effect.

10 or less: You probably have low EI, and find it hard to understand other people or monitor and control your own emotions. This can make social situations a minefield, and relationships difficult. Even though you may be very good at your job, you might not achieve the workplace success you deserve because you're not managing colleagues, bosses, and underlings successfully. In general, the careers that best suit low EI people are solitary jobs or occupations that deal more with things and less with people (e.g., engineering, finance, IT). There's plenty of room for improvement.

Language and Communication

Scoring for Language and communication test

Language ability status test

1: Perfect, 3 points; 1 or 2 mistakes, gets it right second time: 2 points; 3 mistakes, stumbles second time: 1 point.

2: Perfect, 3 points; 1 mistake: 2 points; 2 or 3 mistakes: 1 point.

3: Perfect, 3 points; 1 mistake: 2 points; 2 or 3 mistakes: 1 point.

4: 21 or more: 4 points; 17–20: 3 points; 13–16: 2 points; 12 or less, 1 point.

How did you score?

12–13: Your language skills are sharp. Keep them honed by trying the Challenges on the cards.

8–11: There are a few signs that your language abilities aren't up to scratch. You need to give yourself regular mental workouts—follow the advice in the chapter, and try the Challenges on the cards.

7 or less: Your language skills show marked deficits. Try the test again at a time when you are less tired or stressed. If you get the same score, you may want to examine your diet, lifestyle, or health.

Spelling test

1: unnecessary; 2: assassin; 3: government; 4: rhythm; 5: defendant; 6: (spelled correctly); 7: error; 8: ambassador; 9: indifference; 10: alienation; 11: receipt; 12: (spelled correctly); 13: parliament;14: independent; 15: yacht; 16: sedimentary; 17: eliminate; 18: (spelled correctly); 19: doctrinaire; 20: deference; 21: fuchsia; 22: (spelled correctly); 23: tortoiseshell; 24: (spelled correctly)

How did you score?

Less than 10: Your spelling is bad, which can indicate poor linguistic ability. This may be linked to educational deficits or even dyslexia, but whatever the cause you can overcome it and learn to boost your linguistic abilities.

11–22: You can spell pretty well, but mistakes are creeping in. Some of these may be the result of lapses of memory for spelling rules, while others may be caused by poor linguistic ability. Combine memory and language exercises to make sure you don't make these mistakes in the future.

Full marks: Your spelling is of a high standard but do you know how to use all of those words properly? Practice the exercises and boost your abilities still further.

Understanding IQ

Sample IQ test

Answers

1 DRIP and LEAK

2 45

3

(The black shapes are symmetrical about the vertical axis.)

4 BELT

5 Checking account $600, savings account $1,400

6 SEDATIVE SEDENTARY SEDIMENTARY SEDIMENTATION SEDITIOUS SEDUCTION SEDUCTIVE SEDULOUS

7 CESSATION

8 1 ⅗ (sequence is multiply by 2, divide by 3, multiply by 4, divide by 5, etc.)

9

10 A: − B: ÷ C: + D:

11 STEEP SLEEP BLEEP BLEED BLEND

12

13 ABILITY

14 Second showroom (original prices are $4,000 and $3,500 respectively)

15

16 root/route

17 They both like 13. (Dave likes 4, 7, 10, 13 and Ingrid likes 13, 9, 5, 1.)

18 (The gray circle moves diagonally, the triangle moves along to the right, and so does the black circle.)

19 CHEESEBURGER

20

SCORING:
Score 1 point for each completely correct answer. How did you do? Although it is not possible to use this test to give you an actual IQ score, your score on the test can give you a rough guide as to how you rate compared with the general population.

19–20 Outstanding
17–18 Excellent

14–16 Very good
12–13 Good
8–11 Average

Practice questions

Two-letter words
TP (tepee)
KG (cagey)
AL (ale)
EZ (easy)
RT (arty)
XS (excess)
DK (decay)
NV (envy)
LI (ally)
SA (essay)
YL (while)
XL (excel)
MO (ammo)
CD (seedy)
CL (seal)
FX (effects)
IV (ivy)
JL (jail)
SS (assess)
SQ (askew)

Scores: 4–8 Average; 9–12 Good; 13–16 Very good; 17–20 Outstanding

Alphabetize
a) machinate machiolate macintosh mackerel macramé macrobiotic macrocephalic macrocosm
b) classical classicism classicist classified classless clathrate claudification clause
c) delighted delightful delimit delineate delinquency delinquent deliquesce deliquescence
d) withered wholesome wholehearted whoever whodunit whittlings whittle whither
e) echolocate eclampsia eclectic eclipse eclipsing eclogue ecocide ecology

Wordshare

a) They can all take the prefix MIS-.

b) They all have homophones—words that sound the same but mean different things or are spelled differently.

c) They are all words where the letters are in alphabetical order.

d) All of them require more than just the addition of "S" to make them plural.

e) All of them either mean something else or have homophones that do (e.g., Paul = Pall).

f) They are all collective nouns for groups of animals (lions whales baboons puppies/kittens swallows).

Synonyms

a) OBSCURITY

b) DEBT

c) DELINQUENT

d) DYSPEPTIC

e) LUSH

f) THIN

g) HYPOTHESIS

h) DOUBT

i) CONQUER

j) GELID

Synonyms 2

a) UNSPEAKABLE and INEFFABLE

b) GRATUITOUS and UNNECESSARY

c) DISTANT and REMOVED

Antonyms

a) UNATTAINABLE and CONVENIENT

b) NADIR and ZENITH

c) PINE and DISDAIN

Anagrams

a) HINDRANCE

b) SOMEONE

c) APTITUDE

d) DORMITORY

e) NONCHALANT

f) CROOKED

g) SPLEEN and HEART

h) ALL AT SEA

i) ROCK, COUNTRY, and POP

j) ATTACK and FLEE

k) DOGMA and CREED

l) SET IT UP

Missing words

To enter the speakeasy one had to first find the bogus funeral parlor and then locate and press the hidden buzzer that was secreted behind the spray of lilies in the ornate vase. A gorilla in a suit would pull back the sliding panel and check you out, and if you successfully negotiated this encounter he would activate the mechanism and the whole bier, coffin, and all, would swing back to reveal a flight of stairs.

The key to my educational philosophy, explained the lecturer, is to rationalize the needs of the student with the demands of the examiners, providing all the information the former needs to pass the exams while at the same time stimulating his or her interest in the topic. The course begins by covering the essential aspects of sociology and the first term gives students a thorough grounding in the basics.

Letter change

ALERT	LOINS
AVERT	COINS
OVERT	CORNS
OVERS	CORES
OVENS	CONES
OPENS	HONES
OMENS	HONEY
HEART	THINK
HEARS	CHINK
SEARS	CHICK
STARS	THICK
STARE	TRICK
STORE	TRACK
STONE	TRACE

Letter change 2

ORES R BREW
SEAM E PERK
OPEN P APED
BEAR E FELL
WAND A TAME
FLAT L ALLY

Before and after

a) MAN	k) LIME
b) WORK	l) AGENT
c) FOIL	m) WORD
d) RAIN	n) ROCK
e) CUP	o) CLASS
f) FLOOR	p) STRIP
g) RING	q) HEART
h) SPIN	r) SPRING
i) HORSE	s) CLIP
j) CLOCK	t) PIPE

Investment strategies

Jim: ($1,000 x 70%) x 150% = $1,050.00.
Steve: ($1,000 x 105%) x 105% = $1,102.50.
So Steve has the most.

Bath night

She has 125ml shampoo left, 120ml conditioner left, and 130ml bubble bath left, so she will have to use conditioner first, then the shampoo, and the bubble bath last.

Let them eat cake

9 cakes (Think about the maximum number of one type of cake you can make, and what ingredients that leaves you with. Can you make any of the other types with the remainder? If you swapped a different type of cake for one of the cakes you've already allowed for, would that free up enough to make more cakes of a different type? Can you do this more than once?)

Matter of factorial

a) 45
b) 50/30 = 5/3 or 12/3
c) 18 x 17 x 8/6 = 408

Mirror mirror

$7

Bad start to the day

960 yards

Shapes

Circle = 5 Triangle = 2 Square = 8

Mmmm, pie

a) 2   b) 3
c) 6 (The secret is to avoid cutting across a point where two previous cuts intersect.)

Hex

a)

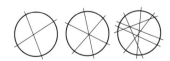

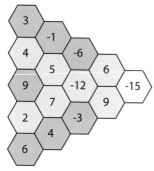

Magic squares

a)

8	1	6
3	5	7
4	9	2

b)

9	6	15	4
3	5	10	16
14	12	7	1
8	11	2	13

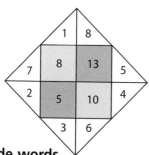

Shopping trip
Three T-shirts, two skirts, two sweaters

Diamonds are forever

c)

1	3	2	5	6	8	4	9	7
9	6	5	2	7	4	1	3	8
7	8	4	3	9	1	6	2	5
4	7	8	1	3	2	5	6	9
5	9	3	8	4	6	7	1	2
2	1	6	7	5	9	8	4	3
3	4	9	6	8	5	2	7	1
8	2	7	4	1	3	9	5	6
6	5	1	9	2	7	3	8	4

d)

8	5	9	6	7	1	2	3	4
1	4	7	3	2	5	6	9	8
3	6	2	8	9	4	1	7	5
2	8	1	7	5	6	9	4	3
7	9	6	4	3	2	8	5	1
4	3	5	1	8	9	7	2	6
9	1	4	5	6	7	3	8	2
6	7	3	2	4	8	5	1	9
5	2	8	9	1	3	4	6	7

Diamond puzzle:

```
      1   8
  7   8  13   5
  2   5  10   4
      3   6
```

Code words
a) 54 (N = 1, B = 2, A = 3)
b) 12 (D = 1, E = 2, G = 3, S = 4)

e)

2	8	6	4	9	7	1	3	5
3	1	4	2	5	8	7	9	6
7	5	9	3	1	6	4	2	8
6	9	2	8	4	5	3	1	7
8	3	7	6	2	1	5	4	9
1	4	5	7	3	9	6	8	2
4	6	3	9	7	2	8	5	1
5	2	8	1	6	4	9	7	3
9	7	1	5	8	3	2	6	4

f)

1	5	2	6	7	3	4	9	8
6	4	9	8	5	2	7	3	1
7	8	3	9	1	4	5	2	6
3	2	8	4	9	1	6	5	7
4	1	7	3	6	5	9	8	2
9	6	5	2	8	7	1	4	3
5	9	6	7	2	8	3	1	4
8	3	1	5	4	6	2	7	9
2	7	4	1	3	9	8	6	5

Memory and Concentration

General Knowledge Quiz

1: Mercury, Venus, Earth, Mars, Jupiter, Saturn, Uranus, Neptune, Pluto (1 point each)

2: World War I: July 1914–November 1918; World War II: September 1939–May 1945 (VE Day)/August 1945 (VJ Day) (1 point for each of the five dates)

3: Continents: Africa, North America, South America, Europe, Asia, Australia, Antarctica. Oceans: Pacific, Atlantic, Indian, Arctic (Southern is optional—don't score for this; 1 point each for others)

4: Comedies are: All's Well That Ends Well; As You Like It; The Comedy of Errors; Cymbeline; Love's Labour's Lost; Measure for Measure; The Merry Wives of Windsor; The Merchant of Venice; A Midsummer Night's Dream; Much Ado About Nothing; Pericles; The Taming of the Shrew; The Tempest; Troilus and Cressida; Twelfth Night; Two Gentlemen of Verona; The Winter's Tale. Histories are: Henry IV, part 1; Henry IV, part 2; Henry V; Henry VI, part 1; Henry VI, part 2; Henry VI, part 3; Henry VIII; King John; Richard II; Richard III. Tragedies are: Antony and Cleopatra; Coriolanus; Hamlet; Julius Caesar; King Lear; Macbeth; Othello; Romeo and Juliet; Timon of Athens; Titus Andronicus (1 point for each)

5: Oslo, Stockholm, Bern, Ottawa, Santiago, Lima, Pretoria, Cairo, Nairobi, Canberra, Kuala Lumpur, Islamabad, Tehran, Kiev (1 point each)

6: Nile, Amazon, Yangtze (Chang Jiang), Mississippi–Missouri (1 point for Nile, Amazon, and Mississippi–Missouri, 2 for Yangtze)

7: I wandered lonely as a cloud
That floats on high o'er vales and hills,
When all at once I saw a crowd,
A host, of golden daffodils (1 point for each line)

8: The sum of the squares of the other two sides (1 point)

9a): Boyle's Law   b): Hooke's Law (2 points each)

How did you score?

Less than 28: Your long-term semantic memory is creaky, either through lack of original encoding (i.e., you weren't paying attention in class) or through poor recall. Improve both your encoding and your powers of recall through practice, and through using the methods outlined in the exercises on the cards.

29–51: Not bad, but there's room for improvement. Again, use the exercises to improve your encoding and recall.

52 or more: You have good long-term semantic memory, which suggests that you are skilled at both encoding and recall. Even if you didn't miss any of the answers, you probably struggled with a few of them, so consider using the exercises to boost your memory powers even more.

Short-term memory quiz

1a: 1 point b: 1 point c: 1 point
2a: 1 point b:1 point c: 2 points
3: If Yes, score1 point
4a :1 point if both b :1 point for each c: 1 point for name,2 for number d: 1 point for name, 2 for number   e: 1 point for name, 3 for number
5a: 1 point if both b: 1 point for each c: 1 point for name, 2 for topic d: 1 point for name, 2 for topic   e: 1 point for name, 3 for topic
6: 1 point for theme, 3 for product

How did you score?

0–10: You have a terrible short-term memory! But don't worry, this book can help—practice the exercises diligently and you can learn the tricks and tactics to boost your short-term memory powers.

11–25: Isn't it surprising how quickly you forget everyday things? Use the exercises to change the way you pay attention to events and retain everyday information.

26 or more: Your short-term memory is good, which probably indicates that you make full use of your senses to maximize your awareness of everyday events, helping you to recall them at short notice. Even if you didn't miss any of the answers, you probably struggled with a few of them, so use the exercises to boost your memory powers.

Brain-boosting Strategies

Caesar cipher challenge

I CAME, I SAW, I CONQUERED

Caesar cipher challenge II

a) Single shift cipher—"All the king's men"
b) Single shift cipher—"Home sweet home"
c) Single shift—"How many roads must a man walk down?"
d) Two-letter shift—"He who laughs last laughs best"
e) Five-letter shift—"Once upon a time"
f) 12-letter shift—"I can't get no satisfaction"
g) 10-letter shift—"In the bleak midwinter"
h) 15-letter shift—"Born in the USA, I was born in the USA"
i) Nine-letter shift—"Top of the world, Ma, top of the world"
j) 21-letter shift—"Ask not for whom the bell tolls"

Follow the instructions

a) J
b) O

Rebus

Manhattan

Rebus II

Citizen Kane

Rebus III

Finding Nemo

Dice game

The probability of it being a tie is 1/6; the probability of it not being a tie is 5/6. The gain if it's a tie is $4; the loss if it's not a tie is −$1. Expected gain = ($4 x 1/6) − ($1 x 5/6) = −$1/6, so Brandon shouldn't play.

Dinner party

a) For six people, there is only one possible arrangement:

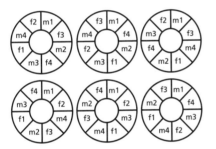

b) For eight people, there are six arrangements:

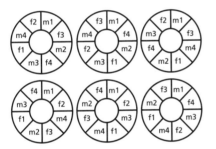

Knight knight

6 moves

5	4	5	4	5	4	5	6
4	3	4	3	4	5	4	5
3	4	3	4	3	4	5	4
2	5	2	3	4	3	4	5
3	2	3	4	3	4	3	4
2	1	4	3	2	3	4	5
3	4	1	2	5	4	3	4
0	3	2	3	2	3	4	5

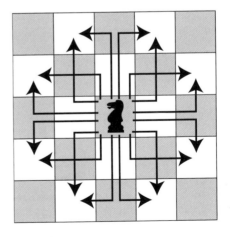

Later, elevator

Started on floor 16, ended up at floor 12. (If A = the floor he started at and B = the floor he ended up at, and you know that A = B + 4, you can work out the number of floors traveled in terms of A and B and then substitute B + 4 to work out A.)

Index